La mística ciudad de Dios (1670)

Scripta Humanistica

Directed by
BRUNO M. DAMIANI
The Catholic University of America

ADVISORY BOARD

La mística ciudad de Dios (1670)
Sor María de Jesús de Agreda

Study and Edition by
Rev. Augustine M. Esposito, O.S.A.

𝔖cripta 𝔥umanistica

62

Esposito, Augustine M.
   La mística ciudad de Dios, 1670 : sor María de Jesús de Agreda : study and edi-
tion / by Augustine M. Esposito.
        p. cm. — (Scripta Humanistica ; 62)
   English and Spanish.
   Includes bibliographical references.
   ISBN 0-916379-67-1 : $39.50
   1. María de Jesús, de Agreda, sor, 1602-1665. Mística ciudad de Dios. 2. Mary,
Blessed Virgin, Saint—Biography. 3. Mary, Blessed Virgin, Saint—Theology. 4.
Christian saints—Palestine—Biography. I. María de Jesús, de Agreda, sor,
1602-1665. Mística ciudad de Dios. II. Title. III. Series : Scripta Humanistica (Series) ;
62.
BT604.M28   1990
232.91—dc20   89-27769
                CIP

                    Publisher and Distributor:
                  SCRIPTA HUMANISTICA
                     1383 Kersey Lane
                 Potomac, Maryland, 20854, U.S.A.

                   © SCRIPTA HUMANISTICA
         Library of Congress Catalog Card Number 89-27769
         International Standard Book Number 0-916379-67-1

              Printed in the United States of America

Dedication

I dedicate this book in loving memory of my sister Marianne
Di Giondomenico who shall forever be remembered and loved!

No movement in religious life has any value unless it be also movement inwards to the "still centre" of your existence where Christ is. It is not what you do that matters most, but what you are.

Pope John Paul II

Acknowledgement

The author wishes to gratefully acknowledge Villonova University for the cooperation received in the publication of this book. Also a word of sincere thanks to Dr. Bruno Damiani for his encouragement and support.

Table of Contents

Introduction

"Come then, my beloved, come. My dove, hiding in the clefts of the rock, in the coverts of the cliff. Show me your face, let me hear your voice; for your voice is sweet and your face is beautiful." (Song of Songs 2:13-14)

1. Statement of Purpose

At first, a vigorous stretch of the imagination may be required to accept the above quote as an appropriate introductory comment to the topic of this book. It might even be regarded as a bit irreverent. Yet, one literary masterpiece often serves as a handmaid to the other. Therefore, the above verse taken from the immortal *Song of Songs* could prove to be at the very least an appropriate antiphon, if not a worthy heralding remark for a study of the work of Sor María de Jesús Agreda. Her recognition as an author is undoubtedly long overdue and the research of her writings lead to the discovery of a literary treasure.

Mística Ciudad de Dios. Milagro de su Omninotencia y abismo de Gracia. Historia Divina y Vida de la Virgen Madre de Dios. Reyna y Señora nuestra María Santísima. Restauradora de la culpa de Eva y Medianera de la Gracia. (1670)

This lengthy title refers to the recordings of a female religious, whose history and background were viewed as somewhat unique, until she became a candidate for sainthood. It appears that often times at this point all mystique

1

and attraction are practically considered normative while at the same time any possible literary contribution is precluded as being of minimal importance. With concern for an appreciation of the literary value of the work of María de Agreda, I would like to direct our attention to the following: Given the fact that Sor María de Jesús de Agreda's most important work of 1670 has not been studied from a literary point of view and that the majority of her related writings remain in manuscript form at the Biblioteca Nacional de Madrid, careful study of that novelesque form, enriched by research in those unedited materials would be a contribution to the study of Spanish baroque literature.

2.Critical Coordinates

It follows, therefore, that I would choose an individual upon whose principles of literary criticism I could confidently base my findings. Mikhail Bakhtin, in my opinion, proves to be such an individual, but not with regard to the obvious, ordinary and readily visible aspects of the La Mística Ciudad. Rather, Bakhtin's expertise will essentially assist in an understanding of that "technical" element of crucial importance which lies at the very heart of the narrative "dynamism" saturating the work, namely, its component of "intertexuality".

Mikhail Bakhtin's studies, findings and theories, which date back to the early 1920's, resulted in decisive contributions to the study of literature, linguistics and language. Collectively, his contributions to literature will have a general bearing upon this study. However, with regard to "intertextuality" in La Mística Ciudad, he will emerge almost as "spiritual director". The combination of Bakhtin and María de Agreda results in an interesting literary chemistry since we will draw from the works of confidence and maturity of each author.

3. Conclusion

Even today, La Mística Ciudad triggers interest for many, in several areas of thought. Yet, it sparked greater interest and created a more serious concern on the part of nearly every seventeenth century theologian for a wide variety of reasons. To this day, the mere mention of communication with heavenly citizens automatically results in confrontation with the Church's scripture scholars, mystical theologians, historians and governing

2

officials. In fact it is virtually unavoidable. So, it followed, therefore, that at the time when one such as Sor María de Agreda was suspected of recording "revelations" as a result of mystical experiences, an extreme ecclesiastical scrutiny of both her and her writings became a forgone conclusion. Today, psychologists, would immediately question the emotional stability of anyone who dares to claim such a virtually inexplicable experience. Once the topic develops into an issue and requires further clarification we soon see the world historian, the sociologist, the physician, the feminist etc. and various other specialists being admitted to the council of Judges assigned to resolve the controversies at hand.

Last, but certainly not least, in order of importance to be called upon for opinion, is the literary critic. Although the social, theological, psychological and historical details regarding Sor María and her work could hardly be considered voluminous, they are at least available and clear. However, the fact remains, that the literary quality of the text has been pitifully ignored. The theologians and psychologists and sociologists have every right to continue to channel their efforts in the direction of their respective concerns. However, excessive dispute would prove unjust as well as foolish if it lead to argumentation concerning Sor María's power of the pen. Doña Emilia Párdo Bazán, an illustrious nineteenth century Spanish author, is quite clear with regard to her appreciation of the "agredista" masterpiece when she comments.

"...la Venerable Madre de Agreda merece figurar entre nuestros clásicos por la limpieza, fuerza y elegancia de la dicción, entre nuestros teólogos por la copia y alteza de la doctrina, entre nuestros escriturarios por la lucidez de la interpretación. Ni son estos los únicos méritos que hacen a María de Agreda digna de glorificación perpetua. Aun prescindiendo de la Mística Ciudad de Dios, la humilde monja franciscana brillaría en la historia y en las letras a título de consejera del rey Felipe IV." (8)

One field of study may choose to consider the work as offensive toward the Church, another, as a behavioral deviance and yet another as some sort of social mishap. The literary critic, however, need only come to appreciate it as a contribution to Spanish baroque literature.

II
Sor María de Jesús

"who is this, arising like the dawn, fair as the moon, resplendent as the sun, terrible as any army with banners." (Song of Songs 6:10)

1. Biographical Notes

The biographies of María de Agreda that are available today, are brief and simple yet describe for us an interesting scenario. Most twentieth century biographical treatment of the Venerable Mother's life appears to be a recapitulation of the sketchy sources made available in the 1800's. Therefore, to truly envision her life would prove nearly impossible without examining the information provided by Fr. Joseph Ximénes Samaniego in his "prólogo" of the 1670 version of *La Mística Ciudad de Dios*. Nearly all writers agree upon basic biographical facts concerning Sor María's life. Actually, it would be more accurate to state that her biographers simply "reiterate" in varying degrees of thoroughness, the information provided by Padre Samaniego in his prologue.

Dependable sources of more comprehensive *bibliographical* information regarding the abbess, would be Luis Alborg, in volume II of his *Historia de La Literatura Española*, Doña Emilia Párdo Bazán's editions of *Vida de La Virgen* (published in 1899), and the conglomeration of authors responsible for the wealth of findings in Vols. 108-109 of *Biblioteca de Autores Españoles* (which primarily contain reference to María de Agreda's famous *Cartas a Felipe IV*. With regard to the aforementioned writers, we must distinguish

4

between what is appropriately considered the scholarly "speculation" of researchers such as Bázan and Alborg and the near "eye-witness" account of the Venerable Mother, of Fr. Joseph Ximénes Samaniego. Collectively, all of these biographers provide information about the Venerable Mother's life which varies from the romantic and nearly celestial to the strictly factual and practically nonchalant.

Without arguing in favor of any one biographer as opposed to the other, I would say that the following facts "collectively" provide a more that adequate summary of the life of the once abbess of the Franciscan convent in Agreda:

María Coronel was born to Francisco Coronel and Catalina Arana on 2, April in the year 1602, in the town of Agreda, belonging to Castilla la Vieja. María is described as having been a holy and prayerful child who did not enjoy particularly good health. The family was not exempt from occasional economic struggles yet, remained well—known and by and large was still considered somewhat influential on a local level. When María reached the age of twelve (this is most interesting to note) the Coronel household is converted into a Franciscan cloistered convent with the consent of the Church, of course.

> "La V. Matrona Catalina, madre de nuestra Doncella María, que ya con la Divina gracia, después de muchos años de vida espiritual, avía llegado a perfectísimo estado de virtud, en uno de estos dias estando en el exercicio de su oración, en que ocupaba tres a quatro horas cada día, fue visitada del Señor con modo muy espiritual. Hablola su Magestad, a sí misma, hijos y hazienda, y que en su casa se edificasse un convento de Religiosas, donde lo fuessen ella, y sus dos hijas, y que su marido entrasse Religiosos, en la Orden de San Francisco eran por disposición del mismo Señor, que con alta providencia prevenía los medios de esta obra." (13-14)

It then followed that María de Agreda' s father and her two brothers sought entrance into a Franciscan monastery while the "future abbess", her mother and sister remained as members of the soon to be canonically established Franciscan Conceptionist abbey. Behind the grails of the cloister, María Coronel becomes "Sor María de Jesús" at the age of eighteen by virtue of profession of vows. Shortly after, Sor María is elected prioress of the community. At twenty-five years of age she is named Abbess of the cloister and served in

5

that capacity until her death in 1665. It is during her appointment as *abbess* that the Venerable Mother composed *La Mística Ciudad de Dios*.

Although one might be convinced that the abbess is deserving of a more impressive biographical account, the fact of the matter is that these few words adequately state all there is to know...at least on a simply factual level. María de Jesús de Agreda's extreme simplicity of life style allows any author to outline her life in so few sentences.

However, it is with great detail and a nearly poetic style in the prologue of Padre Samaniego (1670) that we find greater attention paid to the finer details of her personality and a projectory of her religious life. Fr. Samaniego carefully traces every step of her spiritual development and describes the more trying stages of trial and tribulation for her as religious, abbess and author. A thorough reading of the "prólogo" of Fr. Samaniego in the 1670 version of the text provides tremendous insight into this infamous writing. While the efforts of people such as Bazán and Alborg, whose interests are essentially geared toward literary criticism, Padre Samaniego's concerns are almost exclusively theological. Furthermore, Samaniego's connection with the entire issue of *La Mística Ciudad de Dios* is born out of Holy Obedience to Church authorities and his own religious superiors.

Literary criticism raises intelectually stimulating questions concerning Sor María's writings. For example, was the abbes of Agreda "overshadowed" by Santa Teresa de Avila? What place of prominence would María de Agreda enjoy today had she not been "preceeded" by the paradigmatic mystic Santa Teresa de Avila? Or perhaps equally thought provoking: How much more attention would María de Agreda have received had Spain still believed in mystics at the time of the appearance of *La Mística Ciudad de Dios?* These questions in themselves pave the way for important literary discoveries. However, my purpose here is not to pose one mystic against another or to scold Spain for her lack of faith but rather to concentrate on the undeniably valuable contributions made to the field of Spanish baroque literature as a result of Sor María's work, *La Mística Ciudad de Dios*.

2.   Samaniego's "prólogo", Sor María's biography

It is essential that we re-emphasize the fact that Fr. Samniego's biography of Sor María is determined by the ecclesiastical influence which not only initiated his investigation but in fact demanded it. His relationship with the mystic and the primacy of his role in the investigation of her spiritual journey facilitated the explicitness of detail in his prologue. He was also more capable of providing a very detailed account of María de Agreda's life from a spiritual (and theological) point of view. Once again, were it not for the known fact that Fr. Samaniego carried out this effort toward an expose of her life under Holy Obedience, any reader might presume that his actual goal was to create a "protagonista religiosa" for a work justifiably considered "prosa piadosa".

Fr. Samaniego attests to María Coronel's birth on April 2, 1602 and her baptism on April 11, of the same year.

"En la sagrada fuente la pusieron el nombre de María no sin especial disposición Divina (como despúes manifestó el Señor) para que la que habia de ser especial imitador de la soberana Virgen en las virtudes de su vida, tuviese la inscripción de su sagrado nombre; que por esa providencia se añadió después la contracción "de Jesús", que fue el sobre-nombre glorioso, con que en la primitive Iglesia contrahían los Fieles el nombre propio de la Madre del Salvador llamándola María de Jesús a distinción de las otras Marías." (2)

Almost immediately after the above statement Samaniego relates the strikingly premature "signs" of religious experience in María's life which nearly compels any believing reader to prepare for very saintly charisms to become evident in the life of this child.

"Cuando convalecida del parto salió a Missa, conforme a la ceremonia de la Iglesia, la madre de nuestra Niña ofreciéndola a Dios en su Templo con el afecto que le había ofrecido los otros hijos, sintió tan extraordinario jubílo y consolación en lo interior de su espiritu, que refiriéndolo en su última edad, dezía que ni antes ni después había tenido cosa semejante; y se persuadió que aquella hija venía consignada de la poderosa mano del Señor para cosas grandes de su agrado. Y por esto la Venerable Matrona la crió con más afectuoso cuidado." (2)

Padre Samaniego appears to leave no stone unturned as he scrutinizes María de Agreda's life. Apparently little was concealed from him. Only confessional matters remained a secret in his prologue. At the same time, no consolation, religious experience or heavenly intervention in the life of the Venerable Mother struck him as either insignificant or unworthy of account.

7

We learn from Samaniego, that from her earliest days, María de Agreda was the beneficiary of a wealth of spiritual devotion first practiced by her parents. Also, the very devout catholic Coronel parents considered the value of a high-quality catholic education as incomparable. Although the Coronel children as a group all shared the same educational opportunity, María de Jesús remained singular in what her biographer refers to as "las primeras luces" (in a spiritual sense) which enlightened her to deeply spiritual matters even prior to the initial stages of her formal catholic education. These "first visions" of the future abbess set the stage for a holy drama with the Venerable Mother emerging as the protagonist of unquestionable sanctity (at least from a strictly literary point of view). Holy Mother Church, of course, would comment on the matter from a totally different perspective. Father Samaniego writes:

> "...creció la niña María y antes de llegar a edad capaz de la educación de sus padres, se constituyó Dios por su especial Maestro con prodigiosos favores primero, se habló su entendimiento bañado de Divinas luces en una visión altísima que rayasse en el uso de la razón natural. Fue esta sobrenatural visión el primer conocimiento de esta criatura y Dios el primer objeto que miró. Diósele de improviso capacidad a su entendimiento, fuerzas a su voluntad retentiva a su memoria. Conocí que habia una causa principal de todas las causas, Señor Dios, y Criador del Universo, Conservador y Vivificador de lo que tiene ser. Manifestándolo las miserias humanas en sí misma, con expresión de de todas las circunstancias para formar de si un vagísimo concepto. Pasó a conocer la naturaleza humana en el primer estado de la inocencia, la hermosura, y efectos de la gracia y de los dones Divinos. Y últimamente se le manifestó el estrago que avía hecho en el hombre el pecado, y la fealdad y horribles efectos de mal de los males." (3)

From this point on in Samaniego's biography of María de Agreda, we discover the course of events often typical of the lives of the mystics in all ages. This observation in no way is intended to reduce or simplify her earthly existence to a fairytale-like romance with the Divine in which the Beloved and the beloved "live happily ever after" in the castle of Agreda. Rather in a theological sense, I would say that the remainder of María de Jesús' experiences in the Samaniego prologue recounts a spiritual "kenosis"[1] in a strictly

---

[1]   John A. Hardon, S.J., *Modern Catholic Dictionary*: "The voluntary renuncia-

8

Pauline sense. This "emptying", has traditionally been witnessed by the Church as a pre-requisite to holiness and sainthood as well as mysticism. Sor María de Agreda's relationship with the Divine, in Samaniego's account, resembles the movement of a pendulum swinging between the agony and the ecstacy of surrender to God until the pendulum rests perfectly in the center in silence and peace —which is UNION. Sor María's biography according to Fr. Samaniego can be so easily likened to the joy and sorrow of the Bride in the "Canticle of Canticles" whose joy, although at times is indescribable, hardly escapes from painful longing, severe trial and moments near to the point of despair. In order to see María de Agreda fit hand in glove with the "body of mystics" in the Samaniego prologue, it would be essential to familiarize oneself with the work of The Very Reverend John G. Arintero, entitled *The Mystical Evolution in the Development and Vitality of the Church*. This work is an exceedingly efficient and magnificent historical treatment of the Church's mystics and their experiences. His profound and comprehensive study in conjunction with the conscientious prologue of Fr. Samaniego escorts María de Jesús de Agreda to an undeniable place among the mystics.

Sor María de Jesús remained behind the walls of the cloister until her death in 1665. She single-heartedly devoted herself to God and the sanctification of her spiritual daughters. What preceeded her death, I reiterate, was a beautiful spiritual pilgrimage marked with simplicity of life style. All that could possibly dispute this "simplicity" is a prolonged correspondence with King Felipe IV, another hallmark of the Venerable Mother's collection of writings.

3. *Bibliographical Profile*

María de Agreda's biographical and bibliographical sketch dovetail perfectly. That is, as Fr. Samaniego recounts María's spiritual life, with such detail, a clear vision of the spiritual "progression" of her soul comes into focus for interested readers. Therefore, it comes as no great surprise that the Venerable Mother as abbess, would author truly spiritual works intended for the sanctification of her "daughters" in the cloister. So very similar to Teresa

---

tion by Christ of his right to divine priviledge in humble acceptance of human status. Paul describes 'kenosis' aptly to the Philipians: "His state with God, was divine, yet he did not cling to his equality with God, but emptied himself to assume the condition of a 'slave'. (Phil. 2: 1-6) Greek 'kenosis', an emptying" (302)

de Avila was María de Agreda's aspiration to the "decrease of self" for the sole purpose of an "increase of God", that she too encouraged "spiritual exercises" for all to practice daily in their search for God. The dedicated shepherdess of the flock entrusted to her, wrote primarily for the sake of seeing to it that not one of the sheep should be lost. Her writings serve only to seize every opportunity to foster holiness by urging her "daughters" to make an unconditional surrender of self to the Heavenly Father. Also, according to María de Jesús, the sure touch stone to such a state of sanctity is undoubtedly the Blessed Mother of God. María de Agreda mirrors Augustinian[2] and Teresian[3] spiritual ideals in that her writings reflect a solid commitment to one principal cause for every word she spoke or wrote - the primacy of God (especially in the hearts of her sisters in religion). This cause, won her undivided attention since she considered the pilgrimage of each soul as important as her own. Therefore, regardless of any other God-given talent, a non-negotiable value was placed upon the evangelization of those with whom she had lived, and worked and prayed. This innermost desire is not only obvious but comes to perfection in the following works attributed to María de Jesús de Agreda. They are works charged zealously with the persuit of sanctity:

María de Jesús de Agreda, Mother, 1602-1665. *Mystica ciudad de Dios*, milagro de su omninotencia, abismo de la gracia: historia divina, y vida de la Virgen. Madre de Dios, Reyna y Señora nuestra, María Santíssima, restauradora de la culpa de Eva, y medianera de la gracia. Manifestada en estos últimos siglos por la misma Señora a su esclava sor María de Jesús Madrid: Bernardo de Villa Diego, 1670.

María de Jesús de Agreda, madre, 1602-1665. *Exercicios espirituales de retiro que la V.M. María de Jesús de Agreda practicó y dexó escri-*

---

[2] St. Augustine, *Confessions* IX, I: "How delightful did it instantly become for me to lack the delights of vanities! It became a joy to me to become deprived of those very things which formerly I feared to lose. Thou, O true and Supreme Delight didst cast them from me; Thou didst cast them forth and in their place Thou didst enter in, more sweet than any other pleasure...Then was my mind freed from gnawing cares. and I childlike, I prattled to Thee, my light, my wealth, my salvation, my Lord and my God."

[3] St. Teresa de Avila, *Interior Castle*, sixth mansion, chap. 10: "I was wondering once why Our Lord so dearly loved this virtue of humility; and all of a sudden—without I believe my having previous thought of it — the following reason came into my mind: That is because God is Sovereign Truth and to be humble is to walk in Truth."

tos a sus hijas para que los praticassen en el mísmo religíosisimo Convento de la Puríssima Concepión de la misma villa Madrid: B. de Villa-Nueva, 1718.

María de Jesús de Agreda, madre, 1602-1665. *Ave María. novena. y duodenario de la inmaculada concención de María santísima con consideraciones propias de tan dulce, y soberano mysterio. que para reconocimiento amoroso, y tributo voluntario de la gratitud a la Sacratísima Virgen por el universal patronato de España, sacó de los admirables escritos de la v.m. María de Jesús de Agreda* Madrid: A. Ortega. 1763.

María de Jesús de Agreda, madre, 1602-1665. *Aliento de justos, espejo de perfectos, consuelo de pecadores y fortaleza de flacos en los trabajos de María Santísima, recopilados de la V.M. por María de Jesús de Agreda, por Diego del Valle* Madrid: M. Martin. 1770.

María de Jesús de Agreda, madre, 1602-1665. *Cartas de la Madre Sor María de Agreda y del Rey Don Felipe IV* Madrid: Sucesores de Rivadeneyra, 1885-86.

María de Jesús, a Carmelite nun. *Epistolario de la sierva de Dios sor María de Jesús, carmelita descalza. Illustrado con notas historicas por el R.P. Joaquín de la Sagrada Familia, carmelito descalzo* Toledo: Imprenta de la Editorial Católica Toledana, 1919.

Other works listed in the *Manuscritos Franciscanos de la Biblioteca Nacional de Madrid* are the following: María de Jesús de Agreda, *Leyes del esposo para la esposa.. María de Jesús de Agreda. Obras, 5 volumenes.*

As a "gran finale" with regard to the bibliographical compositions of Sor María de Jesús there must be sounded one last "note" of interest. Actually, I suppose it could appropriately be referred to as an ongoing mutual "arpeggio" between the Venerable Mother and her "earthly" king — Don Felipe IV. "Las Cartas" between Sor María and Felipe IV, serve to inform us of the discord, cachophany and intense dissonence that so harshly interrupted Spain's once perfectly harmonious historical setting. They never betray Sor María's holiness and single-heartedness for God and the heavenly homeland.

The next chapter will provide a "historical score" into which we will place María de Jesús de Agreda — the Spaniard, the abbess and the author.

4. *Historical setting.*

"Order in heaven, order on earth, order even in Hell: men's minds during the Renaissance tended toward such affirmations invariably and often all too insistently. The propensity was by no means a display of excessive piety. It was on the contrary the result of a deepseated, fully experiential awareness that chaos could come again readily enough. Disorder in sixteenth-century Europe was after all a palpable reality, its omnipresence inescapable in the political sphere as in the religious, in the social as in the economic." (Patrides 31)

How fittingly Patrides comments here upon the situation in which Spain found herself as her "Golden Age" began to tarnish with corruption and decline.

Although clouds of darkness began to hover over Spain, and an explosive state of affairs characterized the time in which María de Agreda lived, no one concludes that such chaos played any part whatsoever in the mystic's decision to reproduce the *Historia de la Virgen*. It would be rather ludicrous to even suggest that the critical condition of María de Agreda's beloved "patria" motivated her to any extent with regard to *La Mística Ciudad de Dios*. However, it could be equally foolish to ignore the relationship between the Franciscan nun and Don Felipe IV that developed as a result of Spain's bleak future. Reference here, of course, is made to the infamous and undeniable correspondence between Sor María and the king which apparently lasted for the better part of twenty years. *Las Cartas de Sor María de Jesús de Agreda y Felipe IV* is something without which no bibliographical sketch of María de Jesís would be complete. Nor would any "historical setting" be conclusive without such reference.

One might wonder, was it truly deep rooted faith that prompted the troubled ruler to confide in the "venerable Mother"? Or, was it a "God as a last resort" type of appeal on the part of the mortally wounded and grief-stricken warrior of the Spanish empire? Regardless, in no way is it my purpose to evaluate the relationship between the two avowed citizens of Spain. Nevertheless, even though mention of this "mutual correspondence" brings to a close this brief commentary upon Sor María's bibliographical accomplishments, the doors now open to a clear picture of the Spain's predicament historically.

Stanley G. Payne, in his *History of Spain and Portugal*, outlines the seventeenth century events of Spain, highlighting the essential historical facts without overwhelming the reader with minucia. Payne along with other notable historians, christens the seventeenth century as "the age of decadence and decline." Initial stages of degeneration are first detected in decreased population resulting firstly from the Bubonic plague. Other casualties resulting from epidemic diseases serve as early signs of the great thaw of power. With emigration to America growing in popularity, Spain's population decreased further still. Warfare casualties caused great chunks of the population to fall from the mass of Spain's stability as a whole. These "gaps" left openings for negative waters to seep in and gradually corrode the foundation upon which Spain was to stand firmly for just a short while longer. Soon afterward, the blows of serious economic decline would be felt. In an attempt to explain the prime cause of seventeenth century decline, Jaime Vicens Vives poses a seven part theory. His expertise and scholarly opinion is that the following reasons effectively summarize the causes of Spain's economic decline:

"1) continued increase in the size of entailed domains held by the aristocracy and the Church, which had the effect of withdrawing land from use and of lowering production; 2) increasing social disruption and vagrancy 3) deforestation; 4) an overabundance of clerics; 5) the status orientation of society; 6) the negative, charity oriented religious attitudes toward poverty that precluded serious thought of reform and new enterprise; and most important of all, 7) government policy, which maintained prohibitive taxes in Castile, produced capricious waves of alternating inflation and deflation that led to monetary chaos, overregulated some aspects of the economy, and was incompetent in planning and execution." (292)

Finally, government under Felipe III (1598-1621) also serves as part of the prelude to seventeenth century decline in Spain. By the time of the reign of Felipe III, Spain had already suffered the effects of incompetent monarchs. The insatiable appetite for power and riches of both Felipe III and his "valido" the Duke of Lerma, placed the strain of an additional set of problems upon the royal administration. The results, of course, were the crippling effects of the loss of economic power and security. "As the government bankrupted itself, every device for raising money was snatched at." (307) The result was powerful protest reaching even the upper class citizens.

Felipe IV succeeds his father in 1621. As an interesting aside, we may note that this date coincides closely with the installation of Sor María de Jesús as abbess at Immaculate Conception convent. Both individuals, barely able to be considered of age for their respective "seats" of authority, approach periods of their lives which would prove to be of monumental importance (if on no other level, on a historical one), with the one reigning as king and the other serving as abbess.

Unfortunately for Felipe IV, along with the power of the crown, the sixteen year old king inherits responsibilities which would overwhelm even the most mature teenager. Felipe IV, faced with multitudenous challenges, enters his reign lacking in experience as well as education and equally deficient in a devotion to public affairs. Fate and logic merge under these circumstances and bring forth a thirty-three year old Andalusian noble, who would be known as the Conde Duque of Olivares, upon upon whose leadership the teenage king would depend immensely. Spanish history eulogizes Gaspar de Guzman, (Olivares) as "Duque" for his potential. No historian hesitates to attest to his ambition, energy, vigor, persistence, devotion and respectable absence of personal interests. Yet, despite the powerhouse of hope which Olivares provided, Spain's decline was rapidly and steadily gaining momentum. Stanley Payne concisely summarizes the following four issues as not only contributing factors but also as major, decisive difficulties for Spain and her failing empire:

> a) the size and potential wealth of the overseas empire made it an almost irrestible target for European rivals; b) the extent of the empire's European territories placed it in a dominant position that was eventually intolerable to a revitalized France determined to cut Spain down to size; c) the geographic pattern of the European empire was awkward, for the Low Countries and the French Comite were isolated from the southern base and were difficult to defend; and d) the government refused to recognize the independence of the holy dissident part of the empire, Holland, which had long since broken away and made its own place in the world. (309)

How much can be hoped for under these conditions? What is left once we add to all this the threats and consequences of the Thirty Year's War? It soon began to appear evident that Spain could hardly expect to triumph.

With the final touches of repeated unsuccessful attempts to gain systematic contributions to alleviate her economic defecit and an outright eclipse of the Castillian Cortes the word "decline" falls short of capturing the state of affairs for Spain. Doubt no longer existed. Spain was amid great crises as an empire; her leadership endured agonizing frustrations, its efforts for survival were extremely burdensome and in every regard its economy was a complete disaster. The secession of Portugal from the Spanish crown is just one of the embarrasing testimonies to the state of affairs.

Regardless of how little attention has been paid to the little Franciscan nun-friend of Felipe IV, no historian fails to mention that as the distraught king is left to serve as his chief minister by the illustrious Conde Duque de Olivares, the real and perhaps the only true source of encouragement came from Sor María de Jesús de Agreda, author of *La Mística Ciudad de Dios*.

With regard to Stanley Payne, it should be noted that he is a historian and not a pessimist. Despite the age of decadence and decline he so honestly describes in his work, he still does end on a somewhat positive note:

> "The exception in this general trend of decline was the continued flowering of Hispanic aesthetic culture during the first half of the seventeenth century, when Spain led Europe in the development of baroque art. The painting of Velásquez, the dramas of Calderón and the extravagant poet of Góngora were achievements of the highest level in the European culture of the period. Through the years of mid-century, the prestige of Spanish culture remained high as attested to by the use of Spanish art motifs and the vogue of certain writers, such as the Jesuit Baltasar de Gracián, in France and other countries, Hispanic literature reached its height in the writing of Miguel de Cervantes. His "Don Quijote" was on one level a satire of extravagant and realistic ambitions held by Spanish society of the imperial period and was the most profound expression of the mood of disilusionment that was setting in. On another, it was the most eloquent expression of those ideals, a universal work, and the first modern novel," (306)

The above historical sketch of the seventeenth century may appear to be unduly detailed for our purposes, yet I believe that a fuller picture of the drastic state of affairs lends credence to the fact that Felipe IV frantically sought the counsel of Sor María for her holiness rather than a motive rooted in pure human curiosity. More importantly, the critical study of an important work unaccompanied by its historical setting can often remain incomplete.

15

5. Sor María, the author among Her Contempories

There runs through the lives of many of Spain' s greatest authors a common thread of peculiarity that frequently explains the depth, creativity, inimitable humor, overwhelming pessimism at times, and various other characteristics that won for them great renown. That is, many individual's personal life experiences were woven together into experiences of the extraordinary, thereby clothing them with a sense of awe and at times of the "totally other". This, of course, came to bear heavily upon the power of their stylistic character and thematic thrust. Often, these decisive experiences triggered an appreciation for literature's unique capacity to "capture" and preserve them. Authors were drawn to utilize the power of drama, the novel, poetry and prose literature as patterns to sew together these experiences. The author's soul rather than the pen, often served as the very needle or master tool of the art. In Spanish literature from *La Edad Media* to the twentieth century, authors frequently lead lives that would be superb examples of a captivating drama, novel or short story, in addition to the author's already existing repertoire.

Let us take for example, *El Siglo de Oro* where the incredible folly of love and its limitless misgivings find a perfect dramatization in Tirso de Molino's *Don Juan*. Cervantes' *La Numancia* epitomizes an equally intense perseverance of a "pueblo" in their "lucha hasta la muerte". The undeniable power of man's "libre albedrío" is clearly defined in Amescua's *El esclavo del Demonino*. The absolute farse of man's vanity is unsurpassingly demonstrated in the protagonist of *El lindo Don Diego* by Agustin Moreto while Luís Vélez de Guevarra literally "exposes" the scorn of the so-called "upper class" in his formidable work entitled *El Diablo Conjuelo*. The list of true life experiences or themes echoes like holy titles in the persistent sequence of a sacred litany. These works and others like them prove their power to capture the sting of death, the grandeur of chivalry, the ecstacy of the Divine presence, the enchantment of a woman's beauty, the spell of witchcraft and the undying loyalty of the citizen to the "patria" just to mention a few of those immortal themes which gave Spain her deserved place in literature. This overwhelming "experiential impetus" that so often resulted in Spain's finest works of literature is reminiscent of the "cause and effect" cycle attributed to prophetic literature.

It might prove helpful to make a small analogy at this point between secular literature and prophetic literature. This analogy serves in no way to invite theological argument but rather to clarify and focus a bit more clearly

16

upon the function of Sor María's text. The "phenomenon" of prophecy as treated in the *Jerome Biblical Commentary* refers to a "mediation" and an "interpretation" (of Divine Will, of course). The prophet's intrinsic mission was to direct this knowledge and belief toward others. The "function" was also customarily associated with rational speech and interpretation. The commentary continues by stating: "The means of prophetic communication were in general, the same that are presupposed in Old Testament prophecy dreams visions, ecstatic or mystical experiences and various divinatory practices." (224) María de Jesús resembles the prophets refered to here. That is, she accepts her literary oblitgation toward "others". The only consolation for her amid the burden of writing was that she may somehow share in fostering greater awareness of God and a more complete surrender of self unto Him.

How degrading it would be to these authors of secular literature like Cervantes and many others like him, as well as to the prophets to presume that they merely exaggerated the seriousness of these moments which penetrated their very human existence! The fact that many works are often clear and vivid reflections of the soul of an individual, cannot be denied. Furthermore, the value of these expressions which they have shared with readers is manifest in truths and proverbial knowledge that continue to serve as tools for growth understanding and self-actualization.

Where does the Venerable Mother de Agreda fit in the "anthology" of writers of "experience"? Whom does she preceed? Whom does she follow? Does she belong at all? Reflection upon such questions should yield a more exacting sketch of María de Agreda biographically, bibliographically and historically. I hope to be able to address these questions with specificity on some future occasion. At the moment it is important to proceed with one essential distinction in mind: Sor María de Jesús de Agreda's work contains literary characteristics which always remain "parallel" with others contemporary to her authorship. However these "similarities" never quite converge with those of other authors of her same time period. That is her literary colleagues as well as others mentioned above utilized "experiences" as the spring-board for their literature. The Franciscan nun, on the other hand uses literature as the spring-board for the expression of her "religious experience".

The dynamic among the two types of authors operates in reverse order yet interestingly enough, the result is the same: Both approaches give birth to powerful literary expression.

III
The Text

1. *Narrative techniques vis-a-vis the actual text.*

What transpires, when a reader examines this text, paying due attention to its complexity and beauty? I believe that from the very start of this "historia", (which describes the Conception of Mary) we are quite disarmed by the explicit description of the revealed mysteries they divulge. We are then lured into embarking upon a supernatural journey. Gradually, we feel ourselves falling under the influence of a heavenly trance as we travel through intriguing phases of salvation history. Ultimately we realize that we have been captivated by the "agredista" style in its revelation of historic events which, although well-known on the one hand, appear to be related for the very first time.

María de Agreda has woven multitudes of religious and historical threads into an overwhelmingly beautiful tapestry of the life of the Virgin Mary. Her literary craftsmanship is truly admirable! A brief excerpt carefully selected from the text would prove to be a convincing argument in favor of the text's enchantment. Indeed, a mere highlighting of nearly any portion of the work sheds light upon the authorial expertise to which I have just alluded. Let us proceed further and open the text, listen to its heart beat and examine its "vital organs", so to speak. We must enter into this operation very cautiously, since its anatomy is extremely complex and delicate. The nature of such an operation is not simply exploratory; rather, we are specifically in search of a "structure" and a "technique" that would explain the survival of such prose over the past several hundred years.

What may appear initially as the "Venerable Mother's" humble style, present in her introduction, later flourishes into a recognizable "agredista" technique characterized by magnificent imagery, prayerful dialogue and a sustained celestial tone.

Precisely because of this "agredista" technique, the narration flows pleasantly, progressively, systematically and chronologically. It is consistently coherent with the gospels. The factor which maintains order, clarity and interest to an appreciable extent in an otherwise complex unit of literature is the element of *intertextuality* (which we shall address in more detail in a subsequent chapter). Were it not for this unique facet, the work could have remained to this day a phenomenon merely generating discussion and debate. Intertextuality spares the Venerable Mother's work from being judged as unguided expression and meaningless literary absurdity. It protects her from being accused of employing an undefinable protagonist. It also defends Sor María against the likely impulsive conclusion that what inspired her was primarily schizophrenia or religious neurosis.

The work itself reads like Sacred Scripture. A permeating gentleness enriches her eloquence. Her description is always complete, yet never burdensome, and as a whole the reader is immersed in a peacefully celestial ambiance. Hosts of angels and myriads of heavenly beings continually descend to re-enact the momentous occasions of the Virgin Mary's life:

"Partieron de nazareth para Belén, María purísima y el glorioso san Joseph a los ojos del mundo tan solos, como pobres, y humildes peregrinos, sin que nadie de los mortales los reputase, ni estimasse más de lo que con el tienen grangeado la humildad, ¡Pero, o admirables sacramentos del altíssimo, ocultos a los sobervios y inescrutables para la prudencia carnal! No caminavan solos probres ni despreciados: sino prosperan abundantes, y magníficos. Eran el objeto más digno del Eterno Padre, y de su amor inmenso y lo más estimable de sus ojos. (Col.2:3) Llevavan consigo el tesoro de el cielo, y de la misma divinidad. Veneravalos toda la corte de los ciudadanos celestiales. Reconocian todas las criaturas insensibles la viva, y verdadera arca de el testamento mejor que las aguas de el Jordán a su figura...acompañáronlos los diez mil ángeles...la divina Señora...iba en medio de todos mas oᵘ⁻ ʼnecida y defindida, que el lecho de Salomón con los sesenta ʼnos de Israel lo rodeavan fuera de estos diez mil ángeles asisʼnuchos, que baxan y subían al los cielos embiados del Padre ʼnt. 9:12) a su unigénito humaniado y a su Madre

Santíssima...con este real aparato, oculto a los mortales (salmo 9:12) caminavan María Santíssima e Joseph, seguros de que a sus pies no les ofender la piedra de la tribulacíon porque manda a sus ángeles el Señor que los llevassen en las manos de su defensa y custodia." (*La Mística Ciudad*, Segunda Parte, Libro IV, Cap. IX)

Tenderness and affection add lustre to the literary extravagance and majestic exaggeration which we acknowledge as "baroque" style. The birth of the Virgin Mary as related by Sor María serves as one of the many examples of baroque[1] stylistic beauty:

"Al punto que nació nuestra princessa María, envió el Altíssimo al Santo Archangel Gabriel para que evangelizase a los santos padres del Limbo esta nueva tan alegre para ellos. Y el Embajador celestial bajó luego, ilustrando aquella profunda caverna, y alegrando a los justos que en ella estaban detenidos. Anuncióles como ya comenzaba a amanercer el día de la felicidad eterna, y reparación del linaje humano tan descado y esperado de los santos padres, y prenunciado de los Profetas, porque ya era nacida la que sería Madre del mesías prometido; y que verían luego la salud y la gloria del Altíssimo, y dióles noticia el santo Principe de las excelencias de María santíssima y de lo que la mano del Omnipotente habia comenzado a obrar en ella para que conocieron mejor el dichoso principio de el misterio que daría fin a su prolongado prisíon: con que se alegraron en espíritu todos aquellos padre y profetas, y las demas justos que estaban en el limbo, y con nuevos cánticos alabaron el Señor por este beneficio.

Entró la niña María en las manos de los Angeles en el cielo empíreo, y postrada con el afecto en la presencia del trono real del Altísimo sucedió allí (a nuestro entender) la verdad de lo que antes hizo en figura cuando entrando Betsabé en presencia de su hijo Salomón y desde su trono buscaba al pueblo de Israel se levantó de El,

---

[1] E. Correa Calderón, F. Lárazo Carreter, *Como se comenta un texto literario*: Baroque: Movimiento cultural desarrollado entre 1580 y 1700 aproximadamente. Se caracteriza, en cuanto a las ideas, por un cierto pesimismo y una total desconfianza en los valores humanos; a ello se debe se predomino de obras literarias con caracter moralizador, ascético, o satírico, en esta época. En la expresión, el Barroco ofrece mucha complicación, con exceso de elementos ornamentales (culteranismo) o sin el (conceptismo). Pesimismo y complicación, expresiva pueden darse unidos (Quevedo) pero puede haber uno sin la otra (Argensola, Epistola moral); o, a la inversa, complicación formal con ideología neutra (Góngora). (177)

y recibiendo a su madre la magnificó y honró, dándola haciendo de reino a su lado, lo mismo hizo y mas gloriosa y admirablemente la persona del Verbo Eterno con la niña María que para Madre había escogido, recibiéndola en su trono. Y dándole a su lado la posesión de madre suya y reina de todo lo criado, aunque se hacía figurando ella la dignidad propia y el fin de tan inefables misterios y favores mas para recibirlos fueron sus flacas fuerzas confortabas con la virtud divina. Diéronsele nuevas gracias y dones con que sus potencias respectivamente fueron elevadas; y las interiores sobre nueva gracia y luz con que fueron preparadas, las elevó y proporcionó Dios con el objeto que se la había de manifestar, y dando el lumen necesario desplegó su divinidad, y se le manifestó intuitiva y claramente en grado altísimo; siendo esta vez la primera que aquella alma santísima María vió a la beatísima Trinidad con visión clara y beatifica."

"A los ocho días del nacimiento de la gran multitud de Angeles hermosísimos y regozantes trahían un escudo en que venía grabado brillante y resplandeciente el nombre de MARIA; y manifestándose todos a la dichosa madre Ana, la dijeron: Que el nombre de su hija era el que llevaban allí de MARIA: que la divina Providencia se la había dado, y ordenaba que se le pusiesen luego ella y Joaquín. Llamóle la santa, y confirieron la voluntad de Dios para dar nombre a su hija; y el mas que dichoso padre recibió el nombre con júbilo y devoto afecto. Determinaron convocar a los parientes y a un sacerdote; y con mucha solemnidad y convite suntuoso pusieron María a la recién nacida; y los Angeles lo celebraron con dulcísima y grandiosa música, y solas la oyeron madre y Hija santísima: con que quedo nuestra divina Princesa con nombre, dándosele la santísima Trinidad en el cielo el día que nació, y en la tierra a los ocho días. Escribióse en el arancel de los demas cuando salió su madre al templo a cumplir la ley, como se dirá. Este fue el nuevo parto que hasta entonces ni el mundo le había visto, ni en pura criatura pudo haber otro semejante. Este fue el nacimiento más dichoso que pudo conocer la naturaleza pues ya tuvo una infanta cuya vida de un día no solo fue limpia de las inmundicias del pecado, pero más pura y santa que los supremos Serafines. El nacimiento de moisés fue celebrado por la belleza y elegancia del niño; pero toda era aparente y corruptible. ¡Oh cuán hermosa es nuestra gran Niña! ¡Oh cuán hermosa! Toda es hermosa y suabísima en sus delicias, porque tiene todas las gracias y hermosuras sin que falte alguna. Fue la risa y alegría de la casa de Abrahán el nacimiento de Isaac prometido, y con-

21

cebido de madre estéril; pero no tuvo este parto mayor grandeza que la participada y derivada de nuestra Niña reina, a quien se encaminaba toda aquella tan deseada alegría. Y si aquel parto fue admirable y de tanto gozo para la familia de el Patriarca, porque era como exordio del nacimiento de María dulcísima; en este se deben alegrar el cielo y tierra, pues nace la que ha de restaurar la ruina del cielo y santificar el mundo. Cuando nació Noe, se consoló Lamech su padre, porque aquel hijo sería en cuya cabeza aseguraba Dios la conservación del linaje humano por la area y la restauración de sus ben diciones, desmerecidas por los pecados de los hombres; pero todo esto se hizo porque naciese al mundo esta Niña, que había de ser verdadera Reparadora, siendo juntamente la arca mística que conservó al nuevo y verdadero Noe, y le trajo del cielo para llenar de bendiciones a todos los moradores de la tierra. ¡Oh dichoso parto! ¡Oh alegre nacimiento que eres el mayor beneplácito de todos los siglos pasados para la beatísima Trinidad, gozo para los Angeles, regfrigerio de los pecadores, alegría de los justos, y singular consuelo paralos santos que te aguardaban en el limbo!" (Parte primera, Libro 1, Cap. XXI).

Other captivating moments epressed in equally exquisite baroque fashion are the humility of Mary, her awareness of God's love, an acceptance of and surrender to God as both Daughter of the Most High and Mother of His only Son, the Word Incarnate. Sor María's account of these virtues of the Blessed Virgin, truly focus for us the intensity of baroque stylistic elegance. The unmistakeable theocentric being which clearly defines the Virgin's very existence is so powerful that it almost suggests that the Holy Trinity is the protagonist of the entire work:

"Esposa y paloma mía, prepara tu corazón para que según nuestro beneplácito te hagamos de la plenitud de nuestra ciencia, y para que se escriba en tu alma el Nuevo Testamento y ley santa de mi Unigénito. Fervoriza tus deseos, y aplica tu mente al conocimento y ejecución de nuestra infanta sabiduría determinamos que mi Unigénito, en la humanidad que de ti ha tomado, tenga en una pura criatura la imagen y similitud posible, que sea como efecto y fruto proporcionado a sus merecimientos; y en el sea magnificado y engradecido con digna retribución su santo nombre. Atiende, pues, hija y electa mía, que se te pide de tu parte gran disposición. Prepárate para las obras y misterios de nuestra poderosa diestra.

Señor eterno y Dios inmenso, respondió la humildísima Señora, en vuestra divina y real presencia estoy postrada, conociendo a la vista de vuestro ser infinito el mío tan deshecho que es la misma nada. Reconozco vuestra grandeza y mi pequeñez. Hallome indigna del nombre de esclava vuestra: y por la benignidad con que vuestra clemencia me ha mirado, ofrezco el fruto de mi vientre y vuestro Unigénito; y a su Majestad suplico responda por su indigna Madre y sierra. Preparado está mi corazón y en agradecimiento de vuestras misericordias desfallece, y se deshace en afectos, porque no puede ejecutar las vehemencias de sus anhelos. Pero si hallo gracia en vuestros ojos, hablaré, Señor y Dueño mío, en vuestra presencia, solo para pedir y suplicar a vuestra real Majestad que hagáis en vuestra esclava todo lo que pedís y mandáis: pues nadie puede obrarlo fuera de Vos mismo, Señor y Rey altísimo. Y si de mi parte pedís el corazón libre y rendido, yo le ofrezco para padecer y obedecer a vuestra boluntad hasta morir. Luego la divina Princesa fue llena de nuevas influencias de la divinidad, iluminada, purificada, espirtualizada, y preparada con mayor plenitud del Espíritu Santo que hasta aquel día; porque fue este beneficio muy memorable para la Emperatriz de las alturas. Y aunque todos eran tan encumbrados, y sin ejemplo ni otro símil en las demas criaturas, y por esto cada uno parecía el supremo, y que señalaba el Non plus ultra; pero en la participación de las divinas perfecciones no hay limitación de su parte, si no falta la capacidad de la criatura. Y como esta era grande y crecía más en la Reina del cielo con los mismos favores, disponíase con unos grandes para otros mayores. Y como el poder divino no hallaba óbice que le impidiese, encaminaba todos sus tesoros a depositarlos en el archivo seguro y fidelísimo de María santísima Señora nuestra. (Parte Segunda, Libro V, Cap. VI)

With the gentleness of a sacred, hymn-like descant, we hear the chant of the litany of the August Mother of God, throughout the entire work. The descriptive titles echo, of course, with the added grace of true baroque elegance. Her praises are sung as she is acclaimed "La Princesa del Cielo", "La Divina Esposa", "La Reyna Santíssima", "La Prudentíssima Señora", "Madre verdadera del Eterno Verbo" etc. Sor María's "Historia de la Virgen" reflects more than mere devotion to the Mother of God. More importantly, it is free from error with regard to Vatican II's perception of Mary's role in the Church.[2]

Readers of *La Mística Ciudad* might detect a greater intensity of expression in parts relating the events from the conception of the Virgin Mary up to and including the Crucifixion of her beloved Son. This does not imply, however, any devisive character to the work but simply emphasizes the undeniable depth of powerful stylistic affection which seems to almost sanctify the parts leading to the "Via Crucis".

No one can escape the spiritual dynamic so fully operative in the person of Mary the Virgin. The full impact of her personhood is "experienced" because one not only hears the words she speaks but is also permitted the privilege of listening to the loving dialogue of her heart throughout the work:

"en la oración y ofrecimiento que hizo nuestro Salvador en esta ocasión le imitó y siguió también su Madre Santísima; porque todas las obras de su Hijo santísimo iba mirando en el espejo claro de aquella luz divina con que las conocía, para imitarlas, como muchas veces queda dicho. A la gran Señora iban sirviendo y acompañando los Angeles que la guardaban, manifestándosele en forma humana visible, como el mismo Señor se lo había mandado. Con estos espíritus soberanos iba confiriendo el gran sacramento de su santísimo Hijo, que no podían percibir sus compañeras, ni todas las criaturas humanas. Ellos conocían y ponderaban dignamente el incendio de amor que sin modo ni medida ardía en el corazón purísimo y candídisimo de la Madre, la fuerza con que la llevaban tras de si los ungentos olorosos del amor recíproco de Cristo, su Hijo, Esposo y Redentor. Ellos presentaban al eterno Padre el sacrificio de alabanza y expiación que le ofrecía su Hija única y primogénita entre las criaturas. Y porque todos los mortales ignoraban la grandeza de este beneficio y de la deuda en que los ponía el amor de Cristo nuestro Señor y de su Madre santísima, mandaba la Reina a los santos Angeles que diesen gloria, benedición y honra al Padre, al Hijo y al Espíritu Santo, y todo lo cumplían conforme a la voluntad de un gran Princesa y Señora. (Segunda Parte, Libro XXI, Cap. IX)

"Toda esta visión y sus efectos ordenaba el Altísimo para abrir en

---

[2] Raphael Simon, *Hammer and Fire*: "The teaching of Vatican II on Mary briefly stated, sees her in relation to Christ as His associate in relation to the Church, of which she is the type and the most eminent member; and in relation to us as our Spiritual Mother. She is viewed as the new Eve, as Christ is the new Adam" (40).

el corazón de María las zanjas tan profundas como pedía el edificio que en ella quiera edificar, que tocase hasta la unión substancial y hipostática de la misma Divinidad. Y como la dignidad de Madre de Dios era sin término y de alguna infinidad, convenía que se fundase en una humildad proporcionada, y que fuese ilimitada sin pasar los limites de la razón; pero llegando a lo supremo de la virtud, tanto se humilló la bendita entre las mujeres que la santísima Trinidad quedó como pagada y satisfecha, y (a nuestro modo de entender) obligada a levantarla al grado y dignidad mas eminente entre las criaturas, y más inmediato a la Divinidad; y con este beneplácito la habló su Majestad y la Dijo:

Esposa y paloma mía, grandes son mis deseos de redimir al hombre del pecado, y mi piedad inmensa está como violentada, mientras no desciendo a reparar el mundo; pídeme continuamente estos días con grande afecto la ejecución de estos deseos, y postrada en mi real presencia, no cesen tus peticiones y clamores, para que con efecto descienda el Unigénito del Padre a unirse con la humana naturaleza. A este mandato respondió la divina Princesa, y dijo: Señor y Dios eterno, cuyo es todo el poder y sabiduría, a cuya voluntad nadie puede resistir, ¿Quién impide vuestra omnipotencia? ¿Quién detiene el corriente impetuoso de vuestra divinidad, para no ejecutar vuestro beneplácito en beneficio de todo el linaje humano? Si acaso, amado mío, soy yo el óbice de este impedimento para beneficio tan inmenso, muera primero, que yo resista a vuestro gusto; no puede caer este favor en merecimiento de ninguna criatura: pues no queráis, Dueño y Señor mio, aguardar a que mas lo vengamos a desmerecer. Los pecados de los hombres se multiplican y crecen mas en vuestras ofensas; pues, ¿cómo llegaremos a merecer el mismo bien de que nos hacemos cada día mas indignos? En Vos mismo está, Señor mio, la razón y el motivo de nuestro remedio vuestra bondad infinita, vuestras misericordias sin número os obligan, los gemidos de los Profetas y padres de vuestro pueblo os solicitan, los Santos os desean, los pecadores aguardan, y todos juntos claman; y si yo vil gusanillo no desmerezco vuestra dignación con mis ingratitudes, os suplico a nuestro remedio por vuestra misma gloria." (Libro III, Cap. I)

We see above, how the innermost thoughts and the most profound experiences of the "August Mother of God" are literally unveiled in this work. Yet, in Sacred Scripture we see but a silhouette of a woman who although undoubtedly a key figure, never actually comes into clear focus. Examples such as this, of Sor María's narrative technique are absolutely hypnotic. "Agredista" metaphorical style provides a portrayal of the Virgin which is consistently enriching and inspirational.

We must avoid laboring under the very false impression that the work is dominated by mere religious niceties, unattainable holiness or an undermining of the reality of human life struggles. Foremost are the depths of fear, anxiety and pain experienced by the Virgin Mary as she not only accepts her totally unexpected vocation but grows into an awareness of how "transforming" it actually comes to be for her:

"Como la prudentísima Madre conocía se iban ejecutando los de la redención humana, cuando vió que trataban los ministros de desnudar al Señor para crucificarle, convirtió su espíritu al eterno Padre, y oró de esta manera: Señor mio y Dios eterno, Padre sois de vuestro unigénito Hijo, que por la eterna generación Dios verdadero nació de Dios verdadero, que sois Vos, y por la humana generación nació de mis entrañas, donde le dí leche y sustento, y como al mejor hijo, que jamás pudo nacer de otra criatura, le amo como Madre verdadera, y como Madre tengo derecho natural a su humanidad santísima en la persona que tiene, y nunca vuestra providencia se le negó a quien le tiene y pertenece. Ahora, pues, ofrezco este derecho de Madre, y le pongo en vuestras manos de nuevo, para que vuestro Hijo y mio sea sacrificado por la redención del linaje humano. Recibid, Señor mio, mi aceptable ofrenda y sacrificio, pues no ofreciera tanto, si yo misma fuera sacrificada y padeciera; no solo porque mi Hijo es verdadero Dios y de vuestra sustancia misma, sino también de parte de mi dolor y pena. Porque si yo muriera y se tronaran las suertes, para que su vida santísima se conservara, fuera para mi de grande alivio y satisfación de mis deseos. Esta oración de la gran Reina aceptó el eterno Padre con inefable agrado y complacencia. No se le consintió al patriarca Abrahán mas de la figura y además del sacrificio de su hijo, porque la ejecución y verdad la reservaba el Padre eterno para su Unigénito. Ni tampoco a su madre Sara se le dió cuenta de aquella mística ceremonia, no solo por la pronta obediencia de Abrahán, sino también porque aun esto sólo no se fiaba del amor maternal de Sara, que de paso intentaría impedir el mandato del Señor, aunque era santa y justa. Pero no fue asi María Santísima, aunque era santa y justa. Pero no fue su voluntad eterna, porque con proporción cooperase en el sacrificio de el Unigénito con la misma voluntad del Padre."

Acabada y puesta la obra de la redención humana en su última perfección, era consiguiente, que como el Verbo humanado, por la vida mortal, salió del Padre y vino al mundo, por la muerte de esta vida volviese al Padre con la inmortalidad. Para esto dijo Cristo nuestro Salvador la última palabra: Padre, en tus manos encomiendo mi espíritu. Exclamó y pronunció el Señor estas palabras en voz alta y sonora, que la oyeron los presentes; y para decirlas levantó los ojos al cielo, como quien hablaba con su eterno Padre, y en el último acento entregó su espíritu, volviendo a inclinar la cabeza. Como la virtud divina de estas ultimas palabras fue arruinado y arrojado Lucifer con todos sus demonios en las profundas cavernas del infierno, donde quedaron todos apegados, como diré en el capítulo siguiente. La invencible Reina y Señora de las virtudes penetró altamente todos estos misterios sobre todas las criaturas, como Madre del Salvador y coadjutora de su pasión. Y para que en todo la participase, así como había sentido los dolores correspondientes a los tormentos de su Hijo santísimo, padeció y sintió, quedando viva, los dolores y tormentos que tuvo el Señor en el instante de la muerte. Y aunque ella no murió con efecto, pero fue porque milagrosamente, cuando se había de seguir la muerte, le conservó Dios la vida; siendo este milagro mayor que los demas con que fue confortada en todo el discurso de la pasión. Porque este último dolor fue mas intenso y vivo; y todos cuantos han padecido los mártires y los hombres justiciados desde el principio del mundo, no llegan a los que María santísima padeció y sufrió en la pasión. Preservó la gran Señora al pie de la cruz hasta la tarde, que fue enterrado el sagrado cuerpo (como adelante diré), y en retorno de este último dolor, en especial quedó la purísima Madre más espiritualizada en lo poco que su virginal cuerpo sentía del ser terreno." (Libro VI, Cap. XXII)

I believe it is important to state that María de Agreda never depends upon the fleeting lure of magic, rather, she convincingly emphasizes the Virgin's solidarity with the most Holy Trinity. The Virgin Mary participates fully in even the slightest detail of Divine Revelation, from salvation through Christ to the birth of the Christian Church. Yet, in the text, she could hardly be mistaken for the Saviour. The road leading to this intimate participation is paved by an "agredista" account of the Virgin's unconditional surrender to

the Most High, her never unwavering faith, the purity of her intentions at
every instant and her paradigmatic humility:

"El primer día de esta felicísima novena, sucedió que la Divina
Princesa María después de algun pequeño alivio que recibió. Se
levantó (salmo 45:5) a media noche a imitación de David su padre
(que este era el orden y concierto que le había dada el Señor) y
postrada en la presencia del Altísimo comenzó su acostumbrada oración y santos ejercicios. Hablaronla los santos que la asistían, y la dijeron: Esposa de nuestro Rey y Señor, levántaos, que su Majestad os
llama. Levantóse con fervoroso afecto y respondió: "El Señor manda
que del polvo se levante el polvo." (Libro III, Cap. I)

2. *Narrative Structure*

María de Jesús (co)-narrates the life of the Virgin Mary and begins with
the instant of her conception in the womb of St. Anne. This autobiography-
biography narrates up to and including after the Assumption of "La Virgen",
during which time she assists the four Evangelists in composing the gospels.
This "trajectory" runs parallel to that time period commonly referred to,
theologically, as "Salvation History".

"The heilsgeschichtlich approach views history as a series of redemp-
tive epochs, with the Christ-event as the midpoint of a time line that includes a previous period of preparation, the present stage of the
Church and the eschatological future. All of biblical history is marked
by the permanent tension of promise and fulfillment, the 'already' and
the 'not yet'. Salvation History is thus a characteristic of the whole New
Testament, from Jesus himself to John." (J.B.C. 41:57)

Yet mention need be made of what might be referred to as "pre" and
"post" margins of interest as well as time, concerning the "agredista trajectory". That is, "pre" with regard to the account of the conception of the
Virgin and "post" with regard to the Virgin's assist in the dictation of the
gospels. Neither "margin" is ever commonly included in the definition of
Salvation History.
    There are also definite historical paramaters which are suggestive of an
internal "structure" which would be best illustrated by a triangular configura-

tion. I would identify the "sides" as follows: The work rests upon the foundation of *Prophecy*. From the roots of prophecy stems the salvific event of the *Incarnation*. The triangle is completed by ongoing *Apostolic Mission* directed by the presence of the Most Holy Trinity under the Virgin's patronage. This structural triad seems to encase the name of the work itself and provides sequential logic to its rather lengthy title. In labeling all points of convergence we admit three possible authors of the work: God, the Virgin Mary and María de Jesus de Agreda:

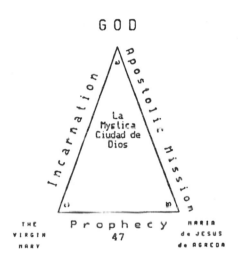

The Venerable Mother, however, is obviously convinced that the true author of her every word is the "August Mother of God". In fact, she writes only because the Queen of Heaven commands her to do so. Therefore, I suggest the above diagram as an attempt to visualize the text, at least in terms of its narrative structure.

J. Halloway seems to value such visualization when he states in his book entitled *Narrative and Structure*, that, in broad terms:

> "narrative comprises events which happen in states of affairs...to talk about structure, on the other hand, is to talk about form in the sense that what one says can be formalized which means that it can in principle be expressed in a formal notation, a symbolism." (5)

Also in keeping with Halloway's train of thought, we might consider *La Mística Ciudad de Dios* as an example of how "structure", according to Halloway, "is what embodies and expresses the deepest and most central idea of the book." (2)

Within the structure just proposed above, the abbess cumulatively creates "revelation within revelation" as she describes the Virgin Mary's reflections upon the carrying out of Jesus' public ministry. She serves him in prayer and adoration whether at his side or separated from him. Similar to a "book within a book", the bible is practically retold by the Venerable Mother of Agreda within *La Mística Ciudad*. Faithful to baroque style as well as to Marion theology, she presents Christ as both *Son* and *King* to the Virgin Mary. There is undoubtedly present in the work devotion and allegiance to the "power of the cross" in its Pauline[3] context. The constant reference to the Old Testament psalms echoes the voice of God's vindication, triumph, promise and dominion. The Crucifixion account is reflective of Markan[4] cristological proclamation in that Christ's identity is revealed in His death by the centurion who pierces his sacred side. It is then carried a step further when the multitude of demons are cast into the abyss as the water and blood pour from the side of thrist, causing an "eclipse" of the Virgin Mother's heart.

"Despedido el Redentor del mundo de la presencia corporal de su amantísima Madre, quedaron los sentidos de la purísima Señora como eclipsados y en obscura sombra, por habérseles traspuesto el claro Sol de justicia que los alumbraba y llenaba de alegría; pero la interior vista de su alma santísima no perdió ni un solo grado de la divina luz que la

---

[3]   John L. Mckenzie, S.J. *Dictionary of the Bible*: The theological symbolism of the cross appears in the NT only in a saying of Jesus Himself and in the writings of Paul. Jesus said that those who follow Him must take up their cross; by this they would lose their life in order to gain it. (Mt. 10:38, 16:24; Mk. 8:34, 9:23; 14:27). This is not only an illusion to his own death, but also a statement that the following of Him demands a "denial of self" and entire disregard for one's own life, personal welfare and personal values, which must be renounced if one wishes to follow Jesus" (162).

[4]   C. F. D. Moule, *The Phenomenon of the New Testament*: "It is difficult to understand how such a presentation of Christ could have seemed adequate, if Mark was really intended primarily as a vehicle of praise and meditation for the worshipping Church. Indeed, Mark provides a striking contrast to what Professor Elinar Molland showed to be the content of Paul..." the content of the Gospel is Jesus Christ Himself. The heart of the Gospel is Christological teaching about the pre-existent One who became man to redeem us, and who suffered death on the cross, and who arose again and is at the right hand of God."

bañaba toda, y leventaba sobre supremo amor de los mas encendidos Serafines. Y como todo empleo principal de sus potencias, en ausencia de la humanidad santísima, había de ser solo el objeto incomparable de la Divinidad, dispuso todas sus ocupaciones de manera, que retirada en su casa sin trato ni comercio de criaturas, pudiese vacar a la contemplación y alabanzas del Señor, y entregarse toda a este ejercicio, oraciones y peticiones para que la doctrina y semilla de la palabra, que el Maestro de la vida habia de sembrar en los corazones humanos, no se malograrse por la dureza de su ingratitud, sino que diese copioso fruto de vida eterna y salud de sus almas. Con la ciencia que tenía de los intentos que llevaba el Verbo humanado, se despidió la prudentísima Señora de hablar a criatura humana, para imitarle en el ayuno y soledad del desierto, como adelante diré; porque en todo fue viva estampa de sus obras, ausente y presente.

En estos ejercicios se ocupó la divina Señora, sola en su casa, los días que su Hijo santísimo estuvo fuera de ella. Eran sus peticiones tan fervorosas, que derramaba lágrimas de sangre, llorando los pecados de los hombres. Hacía genuflexiones y postraciones en tierra mas de doscientas veces cada día; y este ejercicio amó y repitió grandemente toda su vida, como índice de su humildad, caridad, reverencia y culto incomparable; y de esto hablaré muchas veces en el discurso de esta Historia. Con estas obras ayudaba y cooperaba con su Hijo santísimo y nuestro Reparador en la obra de la redención, cuando estaba ausente; y fueron tan poderosas y eficaces con el eterno Padre, que por los méritos de esta purísima Madre y por estar ella un el mundo, olvidó el Señor (a nuestro modo de entender) los pecados de todos los mortales, que entonces desmerecían la predicación y doctrina de su Hijo santísimo. Este íbice quitó María santísima con sus clamores y ferviente caridad. Ella fue la medianera que nos granjeó y mereció el ser enseñados de nuestro Salvador y Maestro, y que nos diese y recibiésemos la ley de el Evangelio de la misma boca de el Redentor. (Segunda Parte, Libro Y, Cap XXIII)

When María de Agreda suggests the formula for holiness and salvation, following it with the admonition against sinfulness and the horror of damnation she clearly reflects the Lucan pericope which relates the famous Beatitudes — and "Woes".[5] The Venerable Mother of Agreda also reflects

---

[5] Raymond E. Brown, S.S., Joseph A. Fitzmyer, S.J., and Roland E. Murphy,

the technique of the Apologetics, in that she addresses lacunae "ad infinitum".[6] A mere glance at the titles of each chapter attest to these "lacunae" and at the same time rouses our curiosity. (10)

Of course, from a more secular point of view (which still remains as my purpose) she can also be acknowledged for satisfying anyone's curiosity for facts not related in the Sacred Scriptures.

Indeed a study in itself would be necessary to comprehensively appendix the historical facts, Christian beliefs, salvific implications and religious mysteries that the Venerable Mother brings to life in her work. Yet, perhaps a more accurate summary comment would be that collectively these facts and beliefs were and still remain an integral part of the structure of the Roman Catholic Church. Even discarding concern for religious truths motivated by faith, we cannot fail to appreciate how this narrative so confidently describes the birth of the Apostles Creed, the manner in which the division of territory of the world took place for evangelization by the Apostles, the heavenly triumph over all the demons of hell as the Messiah fulfilled His salvific mission and the private prayers of the Virgin Mary etc. Moreover, the "cast" of characters for the entire story is comprised not only of the Old Testament patriarchs and New Testament prophets but more importantly includes the three members of the Blessed Trinity and the Queen of heaven and earth.

3. *Intertextuality*

> "One could praise Mikhail Bakktin, without too many qualms, on two accounts: that he is the most important Soviet thinker in the human sciences and the greatest theoretician of literature in the twentieth century. (The Dialogical Principle, 32)

Mikhail Bakhtin, despite his great interest in religious subjects, never wrote about *La Mística Ciudad de Dios*. Yet, his literary scholarship and ex-

---

O. Carm., *The Jerome Biblical Commentary*: "While Mt. has nine beatitudes and no 'woes', Luke has four of each. Luke not only rearranges the sequence of the beatitudes from Matthew's first, fourth, second and last; but the 'woes' follow the reverse pattern of the beatitudes. Such stylistic patterns are typical of Luke" (135).

[6] John A. Hardon, S.J.: "Apologetics — the science that aims to explain and justify religious doctrine. It shows the reasonableness of such doctrine in the face of the objections offered by those who refuse to accept any religion, especially Christianity and more particularly Roman Catholicism" (34).

pertise lead us to an understanding of the very characteristics that renders the seventeenth- century prose work worthy of recognition. Through his conscientious treatment of what he calls "The Dialogical Principle", we awaken to the true mystique of La Mística Ciudad de Dios.

Personally, I prefer to consider the development of his "principle", as a "transfiguration" of the work which otherwise might still be considered unimpressive if not altogether unknown.

Mikhail Bakhtin, as a theoretician of texts whose interests extend even beyond literature, has devoted a considerable amount of effort in an attempt to understand, exlain and situate the value of "utterance". He defines it, at least in part, as:

> "The product of a working up, in which linguistic matter is but one of the ingredients; another is all that is brought to a verbal production by the fact of it being uttered, that is its unigue historical, social, cultural context. (26)

Bakhtin repeatedly makes an issue of the fact that "the most important feature of the utterance, or at least the most neglected, is its dialogism, that is its intertextual dimension." (X) Even though we might at first fail to see any significant connection here between these "concepts" of the Soviet thinker and the "visions" of the Spanish mystic, I found greater understanding of the latter's work and cause for deeper appreciation of its content once such a connection was made.

Bakhtin's interests, as a whole, are basically divided into four major areas: Epistemology, Translinguistics, History of literature and Philosophical Anthropology, "... and the dialogical principle remains his dominant theme, whatever the object object of scrutiny." (13) The word "scrutiny" here is what will lead us into an appreciation of and for Bakhtin's contribution to all literary criticism, and in particular to that of the "Historia de la Virgen". We must allow ourselves to be honestly confronted with some sobering (scrutinizing) questions: What truly appreciable literary technique, characteristic or device is contained in this voluminous "Vida de la Virgen"? Granted, María de Agreda writes the mystifying story of the life of Mary, the Mother of God. Indeed, angels and devils, prophets and saints, apostles and martyrs fill the numerous chapters of her books. But, as was stated earlier, have we not seen an abundance of equally interesting and entertaining features in many a Spanish author's work both long before and years after the appearance of the Venerable Mother's version of the Virgin Mary's life? Are we compeled to applaud the abbess merely because she includes the Holy Trinity among her cast of characters? Or, do we singularize her work simply because she retells "the greatest story ever told"? There must be something more specific, (if not unique), to captivate interest and gain literary recognition for this seventeenth century work of prose. The answer, I believe, lies in an understanding of what Bakhtin concludes is the "Dialogical Principle".

As readers of *La Mística Ciudad de Dios* we actually become privy to a "dialogue", a mystical dialogue in which the "utterances" alternate (or are at least exchanged) between the human and the divine. The "dialogism" in this case ultimately resulted in written form as the History of the life of the Virgin Mary. As a text, it contains all of the typically enriching ingredients of appealing baroque literature. "Personalization", "subjectivity", and "ideology" and of course "intertextuality" in authentic Bakhtinian terminology are at their best in *La Mística Ciudad*.

"At the most elementary level", Bakhtin tells us, "any and all relations between two utterances are intertextual". (60) It is with this "elementary" remark, that Bakhtin begins to unveil the true narrative technique hiding beneath the fascination and mysteriousness of María de Agreda's "revelations". The unveiling continues as Bakhtin fleshes out the meaning of "utterance". He states:

> "In order to become dialoaical, logical relations and objectal semantic relations must achieve material existence, as was said earlier, that is they must enter into another sphere of being: become discourse, that is utterance and receive an author whom we hear in the very utterance as its creator." (61)

He adds further:

> "This does not mean, it will be recalled, that the utterance gives expression to the inimitable individuality of its author. The utterance at hand is perceived rather, as the manifestation of a conception of a world while the absent one as that of another conception; *the dialoaue takes place between the two*." (61)

At last, the captivating mystery of Sor María's work is at least envisioned if not yet totally grasped by understanding. That is, it would not be accurate or fair to presume as readers that María de Agreda in any way completely controls or determines the dialogue, interaction, course of events or exactitude of detail of her text. Rather, the role which the virgin plays within and outside of the text (which is in fact the "absent" or the "another conception" to which Bakhtin refers) is dynamically present and even adds an air of suspense as to how the "Historia" will unfold or be revealed. The chain of "Doctrinas de la Reyna del cielo María Santísima" acting as "literary seams" best illustrates the "other" or "absent" dimension of the dialogue (dialogism) in the work. These "doctrinas" distinctly create a space, or a pause between the two "interlocutors" so to speak, who are engaged in this dialogue. Again, once readers are immersed into this technique (even if they not be fully aware of it) they enter into the rythm of the conversation set forth by this narrative technique. At this point the reader begins to almost "walk" through the years of time related in the "historia".

One might argue over the validity of two individual and separate dialoguing partners here. It may very well be debated as to whether María de Agreda is independently established at all or whether she is merely recording secretary to the Virgin Mother of God. However, we must not fail to recognize that as a mystic, the disposition of her heart is the first response to the initial "utterance" of the Beloved, responsible for the dialogue of souls. Let us recall how Bakhtin cautions that the utterance does not necessarily give expression to the inimitable individuality of its author but simply is perceived as the manifestation of a "conception" of the world. Again, he reiterates that "dialogue" takes place between the two. When listing his prerequisites concerning dialogue and discourse, Bakhtin concludes by saying, "The dialogical reaction endows with personhood the utterance to which it reacts". (61) This comment not only provides closure for Bakhtin's non-negotiable concepts with regard to dialogue and discourse but at the same time focuses very clearly for us a most important feature of the dialogical principle and its role in elucidating the Venerable Mother's narrative technique. Such "endowing" places the persons of María de Agreda as well as María la Virgen — within our reach! If truly attentive to and aware of the "dialogical principle" we acquire the ability to visualize the personhood or personhoods in their shared dialogues of joy, sorrow, anxiety, hope and despair at times, that are relived, recorded and communicated in the work. This very "personhood" frees us (at least some of us) from being caught in the web of concern over dogmatic validity and revelatory accuracy. At the same time, it allows all readers to enter into the "contenido" of a text in whose technique, style and character are found the power and delights of literature at its best.

The following theories and concepts of Bakhtin gradually complete the

35

"unveiling" process and expose the literary refinements made by the dialogical principle. In a rather general yet convincing statement, Bakhtin seems to argue that the environment and setting of Sor María's work are credible rather than extraordinary or ridiculous. He states:

> "Every representation of language puts us in contact with its utterer: to make us conscious of what language is, is to have us identify who speaks within it. This "personhood" covers the gammut from an entire linguistic community...to the subject of individual forms of expression and passing through the subject of dialects and styles in all their variety." (62)

La Mística Ciudad de Dios bears witness to the Bakhtinian theory which contends that: "In the authentic novel, one can feel behind every utterance the nature of social languages with their internal logic and necessity. The image of such language in the novel is the image of the social horizon, of the social ideologeme, welded to its discourse, to its language." "(62) These concepts are truly epitomized in the tone, style and spirit of María de Agreda's work.

Bakntin further supports his theory when he distinguishes "prose" from "poetry" using the very element of intertextuality to separate the two:

> "It isn't that the representation of discourse, and therefore of its utterer, is impossible in poetry, but it just isn't aesthetically valorized there as it is in prose. Most poetic genres (in fact the strict sense of the term) do not avail themselves of the internal dialogism of discourse artistically; it does not enter into the "aesthetic object' of the work; it is conventionally stifled in poetic discourse. In the novel, on the other hand, it becomes one of the most essential features of prosaic style, and receives a specific artistic elaboration." (64)

It is precisely in this very same area of interest that Bakhtin brings *La Mística Ciudad de Dios* to mind. He emphasizes how the prose writer (as opposed to the poet) never weds himself to any given language. Rather, he speaks "through" language.

Certainly María de Agreda's caution and even adversity, at times, to her own writing would not convince us that she intentionally chose a specific type of language for the sake of defending her personal argument for the course of events in the life of the Virgin:

"Confiésote y magnifícote, Rey Altísimo, que por tu indignación y levantada majestad encubristes de los sabios y maestros estos altos misterios, y los revelastes a mí, tu esclava, la más párvula e inútil de tu iglesia, para que con admiración seas conocido por todopoderoso y autor de esta obra, tanto mas cuanto el instrumento, es más vil y flaco". (Mt.22:25) (Primera Parte, Libro III, tap. XI)

From a strictly theoretical approach to literature, over and above his argument concerning "utterance", Bakhtin defines several terms which I believe are essential to an understanding of María de Agreda's work. They highlight the text as literature rather than Sacred Scripture, Church dogma or exclusive Catholic devotion. These terms are: "ideology", "understanding", "personalization" and of course, "intertextuality", which we have just addressed.

He speaks of "ideology" as follows:

"The set of reflections and refractions of social and natural reality that is held by the human brain and which the brain expresses and fixes through words, drawings, lines or whatever signifying (znahovoj) form. (17:53). Ideology: that is in a sign, a word, a gesture, a graph, a symbol, etc." (18)

If we agree in any way at all with this definition of ideology, we would also concur with the idea that it would be nearly impossible to overlook or deny in Sor María's work, definite religious life principles and an awareness of the seriousness of the matters she related. It would be even more of a challenge to dispute the fact that the "personalization" in her work is as Bakhtin states: "..... in no way subjective or that the boundry there is not the "I" but this "I" in interrelation with other persons, that is the I and the other, I and thou." (19)

A final idea of Bakhtin I wish to include here is one that simply cannot be overlooked at this point, yet may require an attitude already disposed to Bakhtin's theories in general. Nevertheless, I believe that it is essential to a more complete understanding of the Soviet thinker's true contribution to a study of La Mística Ciudad. When speaking of epistimology of the human sciences, he describes "understanding" as a "transposition that keeps non-fused two autonomous consciousnesses." (22) Since "understanding" is the guiding light and life-giving principle to the narrative of María de Agreda, it would be best to quote at length from Bakhtin's thinking in order for us to visualize how undeniably operative his principles actually are within *La Mística Ciudad de Dios*.

"It will be no surprise that to such a radical difference in the object there should correspond a difference of method: Bakhtin prefers, in fact, to speak of understanding with respect to the human sciences rather than knowledge, thus faithfully following the tradition of Dilthey, Ridkert, and Max Weber, already in the writings of his youth, on the occasion of an attack against the aesthetics and epistimology of empathe (ein-fuhlung), Bakhtin describes understanding as a transposition that keeps nonfused two autonomous consciousnesses.

In its naive and realistic interpretation the word "understanding" always induces into error, it is not at all a question of an exact and passive reflexion, of a redoubling of the others experience within me (such a redoubling is in any case, impossible) but, a matter of translating the experience into an altogether different axiological perspective, into new categories of evaluation and formation.

In subsequent writings, he will particularly stress the irreducible duality of utterer and receiver, the first characteristic feature of understanding is that it tends to take the form of a reply elicited by the initial remark (the object to be known).

All true understanding is active and already represents the embryo of an answer. Only active understanding can apprehend the theme (the meaning of the utterance) it is only by means of becoming that becoming can be apprehended... All understanding is dialogical. Understanding is opposed to utterance like the reply is opposed to another within a dialogue. Understanding is in search of a counter-discourse to the discourse of the utterer. (12:122-3)

There is no difference of nature here between the knowing discourse and the discourse to be known: They are co-substancial, some thing that is obviously not the case as far as the natural sciences are concerned.

Thoughts upon thoughts, experiences of experiences, discourse upon discourses, texts upon texts, therein lies the fundamental particularity of our (humanistic) disciplines by opposition to the natural sciences, although there too, there are no absolute or impenetrable boundries (30:281).

Logically, one can certainly distinguish between language and metalanguage, text and metatext, but for Bakhtin, the metatext relation is not specific: the metatext is actually an intertext: the utterance that describes another utterance enters into a dialogical relation with it... *it is encounter of two subjects, two authors.*" (22-23)

In light of what has just been quoted from Bakhtin's Dilogical Principle, let us consider the following excerpt from La Mística Ciudad by Sor María de Agreda:

> "Hija mía, muchas veces en el discurso de tu vida, y mas en este tiempo *que escribes la mía*, te he llamado y convidado para que me sigas por la invitación mayor que tus fuerzas pudieran con la divina gracia, ahora de nuevo te intimo esta obligación y llamamiento despues que la dignación del altísimo te ha dado inteligencia y luz tan clara del sacramento que su brazo poderoso obra en mi corazón, escribiendo en el toda la ley de gracia y doctrina de su evangelio y el efecto que hizo en mi este beneficio, y el modo con que yo lo agradecí y correspondí en la imitación adecuada y perfectísima de mi santísimo hijo y maestro." (Segunda Parte, Libro V, Cap. VI).

This brief chapter is in no way proposed as exhaustive with regard to Bakhtin's dialogical principle and its operative component in La Mística Ciudad de Dios. Rather, it serves as a mere introduction to the depth of Bakhtin's theoretical understanding which so ingeniously conceives a "principle" that can be recognized by us as an underlying operative element in Sor María's text.

4. Polemics of the 17th and 18th centuries

It is indeed a testimony to the inadequacy of words to say that a "polemic" resulted from this work of Sor María de Jesús de Agreda. It is precisely the seventeenth and eighteenth centuries that witnessed the most memorable days of what seemed to be outright war waged between "agredistas" and "antiagredistas". The theological judgements regarding the controversial text recorded by Fiscar Morison in his English translation of 1914 include those of the Augustinians, Benedictines, Carmelites, Domenicans, Jesuits, Cistercians, Basilians, Trinitarians, Mercedarians, Mimims, Herionymites, Premostratensians, Reformed Augustinians, Theatines and

Minors of the regular clergy. (XIII) The scanty commentaries on the work of the Venerable Mother fail to make mention of rigorous Inquisitional opposition to her work. This scrutiny by the Religious Orders began shortly after the death of María de Jesús and lasted for over twelve years before any valid approval was made public in 1686. However, final approval was still a long way off. Extremely opposite views would collide and deeply rooted disagreement would begin to sprout and flourish rapidly. *What the Universities of Europe, the Religious Orders and learned men say of the Ciudad de Dios*, published in 1914 and translated by Fiscar Morison provides detailed recordings of this series of conflicting edicts concerning the work from the seventeenth century to the nineteenth century. The issue of María de Agreda's work reached a particularly intense level of interest and concern in the eighteenth century. The end of that same century remains as the time period during which one could then confidently refer to an actual war waged between *strongly opposed* "agredista" parties. In fact, an appreciation of *La Mística Ciudad de Dios* suffered greatly from prolonged insoluble conflicts over the work which lasted throughout most of the eighteenth century. This confusion nurtured itself upon repeated propositions, apologies and inpugnations concerning the work. It seems as though the recommendation of September 29, 1885 by Bishop Ignatius of Ratisbon most accurately summarizes the approbation that echoed in the Church until the last and final word spoken "ex-cathedra" in the year 1912. After a summation of the decrees of Pope Innocent XI (1686) and Clement XI and several others, the concluding statement of the decree announced the following:

> "I therefore, do not hesitate—in granting our Episcopal approbation to—*Ciudad de Dios*—and wish to recommend it to the faithful and especially to our clergy." Franz Albert, Archbishop. (1885) (XX)

Before this final approval was decreed, the work of Sor María de Jesús was repeatedly moved on and off the index of condemned books in the Catholic Church. To this day, nearly every available English text in connection with the *Mística Ciudad de Dios* provides for readers a comprehensive summary of the list of approbations connected with the work. The slightest review of the scrutiny of her work easily convinces the reader that the "time and topic" were hardly compatible with an "era" that had no appreciation for even the most insignificant resemblance of a theological "error".

Recordings indicate that not all Bishops became equally enamoured by the "Historia de la Virgen" and this of course, gave way to controversy of great significance especially after papal approval of the work had been won by the "agredistas". Naturally, with the cannonization process already underway, just eleven years after the Venerable Mother's death in 1665, every word of the abbess would be subject to doubt, question, scrutiny and suspicion. Yet, in spite of the typical opposition, the seventeenth and eighteenth centuries were clearly marked with increasing popularity and appreciation for the already esteemed work of the abbess. Translation of the work into many other languages would become available long before the turn of the nineteenth century. With the dawning of the nineteen hundreds, we see a clear vision of the great esteem won by this work. Approbations (see appendix III) will clearly show us how impressive the members of the Venerable Mothers council of Judges were. We shall see as well, that the Church did not hesitate to avail herself of the most apt and qualified of examiners, to test this nearly blasphemous title: *La Historia de la Vida de la Virgen María!*

Before we leave the sacred chambers of the Ciudad de Dios we must first tie the loose ends that remain with regard to the whole truth concerning the "polemics", which were occasioned by the text. Choosing the word "polemic" to describe the repercussions of this work is both fair and appropriate. However, limiting controversy to the "outside world" would be unjust and inappropriate indeed! Although Church History attests to the seriousness of events connected with the appearance of Sor María's writings, we need to return to chapters 23, 32, 35 and 45 of Padre Samaniego's prologue (references below) for a complete testimony to "polemics". As outside forces and authorities waged war upon the work, severe attacks from "within" constantly fell upon the author herself. What is of even greater importance is that these same chapters further indicate the authentic purpose and spirit of María de Jesús de Agreda:

"Dispuesta, pues, María de Jesús, con la elevación del espíritu, con la asistencia de los Angeles con la comunicación de las Vírgenes, con el magisterio de la Reyna Madre con la infusión de la ciencia, con la perfección de Esposa, con los brazos de su Esposo Rey, y últimamente con los ardientes deseos de la salud de las almas, herencia de su Esposo, adquirida con su sangre; se le intimaron de nuevo los mandatos de escribir, para enseñanza propia, gloria de Dios, honra de su Madre, y aprovechamiento de los Fieles, la Divina Historia, y descripción de la Mystica Ciudad de Dios María Santísima con tan apretada instancia y clara manifestación de ser essa la voluntad Divina..." (Cap. XXIII)

The above quote although seemingly off the track, actually sets the stage for the controversial drama to follow. Chapter 23, in the 1670 version compliments the opening statement of the text: "...comenzó la V. Madre de Jesús a escribir la Vida, y Historia de la Reyna de los Angeles en el año del Señor 1637." (Cap. XXIII) Further on we discover that an apparent passion motivated Sor María to such an extent that: "Y en este encerramento en solos veinte dias escribí toda la Primera Parte de la Historia; siendo tanta la influencia de la luz Divina". (Cap XXIII) A least likely expected ingredient of the "polemic" appears in this same chapter (23) of the prologue of Samaniego and gradually becomes an element not only of the polemic in discussion at this point but of the very text of the "Historia" itself: ..."al Demonio de oponerle con todas sins astucias, y combates para el exercicio de su Sierva..." (Cap. XXXV) It is "El Demonio" who will remain very present both inside and outside of the text.

In chapter 32 of the prologue we advance to an even greater understanding of "La Historia" amid many problematic encounters. Once again, the polemic results in religious scrutiny, moral scrupulosity, the voice of Church authority and in what today would incite a riot among the supporters of the feminist movement:

"Al fin de efecto, que hallándose este Confessor con el gobierno de la V. Madre, la dijo que las mugeres no avían de escribir, y que asi el la mandaba por obedencia quemasse la Historia de nuestra Señora. Y otro qualquier tratado que le hubiesse mandado, que escribiera." (Cap. XXXV)

The venerable Mother, of course, immediately obeys her substitute confessor. Actually, she was totally relieved by his orders. Unfortunately, her relief was quite short-lived. Very soon afterward, this decision is reversed and she will write once again:

"Asi se lo revelaron los Santos Angeles, diziéndola, que avía años que avía de aver muerto y que el Señor le concedí la vida para que escribiesse segunda vez la Historia de Su Madre Santíssima. (Cap. XXXV)

The venerable Mother enters into her own personal and nearly exclusive polemic: "Sin Majestad Divina le concedió al Infernal Dragon la pelea, y que a ella la prevenía para padecer mucho." (Segunda Parte, Libro IV, Cap. IX)

Perhaps the attention given here appears to be trivial or merely "behind the scenes" religious life nonsense. However, it could be argued that the more decisive polemic occasioned by the work of the Mother Abbess surfaces precisely in these very events just mentioned. Were it not for the final resolution of these "cloistered polemics", however, the world may never ever have heard of the life of the Virgin Mary by Sor María de Jesús de Agreda.

5. Twentieth century "obscurity"

To state that the Venerable Mother's work in the twentieth century is considered "obscure" at best would create no real dispute. An investigation of María de Agreda as a historical figure would probably spark much greater intrest than one of María (Coronel) de Jesús the author of *La Mística Ciudad de Dios*. She cannot be forgotten, at least historically, for the simple reason that the king of Spain initiated a lasting correspondence with her. It remains true that it was indeed more credible that Sor María maintained Felipe IV as a frequent correspondent and counselee rather than the Blessed Virgin Mary as daily companion, divine mediator and personal narrator of her own life's story. In simple ordinary terms, with regard to Sor María de Jesús de Agreda and her supposedly infamous "obra literaria", very few anthologies even make mention of her. If there be any such mention, *La Mística Ciudad de Dios* seems to enter into the picture with care and caution while *Las Cartas a Felipe IV* are addressed with very little reserve at all. In fact, they become the focal point of interest in her case.

Among the five groups or schools of Spanish mystics (Dominican, Franciscan, Carmelite, Augustinian and Jesuit) María de Jesús de Agreda still remains virtually unacclaimed. Yet, in her writing, she clearly reflects the depth and enchantment of two of the more commonly referred to among these "schools", namely Santa Teresa de Avila and Fray Luís de León. María de Jesús de Agreda reminds us of the Augustinian monk significantly, in that her work overflows with harmony, musicality, stylistic precision, a profundity of ideas, a coherence that underlies all chaos of phenomenon, a christocentric vision and a brutal contrast between man and the divine. Oddly enough, however, Fray Luís de León and Sor María de Jesús differ greatly in that the Venerable Mother breathes neither pain nor nostalgia into her work for a desired harmony which she cannot attain. No search of "perfect form" characterized her text nor does she find herself lured into the "campo" for a reprieve from any personal "inquietudes" that overwhelm her.

43

María de Agreda does evidence a lively "espontaneidad" which is definitely "teresian", yet her genre could hardly be precisely categorized as "epistolary" as is that of Teresa de Avila. One cannot deny that both of these female Spanish mystics here deserve recognition and manifest a desire for linguistic precision and exactitude. Yet, while a Teresian hallmark is obviously that of "imagery" and the multiplication of synonyms, Sor María differs from her Carmelite sister mystic in *La Mística Ciudad* in a rather significant way. That is, Santa Teresa de Avila's technique shows a tremendous dependence upon "la comparación". Sor María's narrative character, on the other hand, comes into being from a plain and simple attempt to "relatar una historia" unto the very end.

When Luis Alborg discusses the works of San Juan de la Cruz, he uses the term "meditación discursiva". Although such a phrase may accurately describe the spiritual benefit of a reading of this work by Sor María de Jesús de Agreda, it is still somewhat out of kilter with the "agredista" text as a seventeenth-century prose work.

In conclusion, we must acknowledge the style and technique of prominent mystical authors as helpful guides and valuable points of reference with regard to María de Agreda's work. However, in my opinion, it still appears more exacting to consider the Venerable Mother's narrative technique as truly her own. That is, uniquely and authentically — "agreditsa"!

"Come then my love, my lovely one come, my dove hiding in the clefts of the rock, in the coverts of the cliff, show me your face, let me hear your voice, for your voice is sweet and and your face is beautiful."
(Song of Songs 2:13-14)

44

IV
Conclusions

Indeed our undivided attention is required if we are to ever arrive at any intelligible conclusions regarding the narrative technique of María de Agreda's *La Mística Ciudad de Dios.* In fact, even an intense concentration upon the work may never describe, with reasonable accuracy, exactly what is meant by the narrative technique of the "venerable Mother". I could simple state that her narrative technique is complex and beautiful. However, even if there were any value at all in such a trite comment, we would at best suffer from a terrible lack of appreciation for the text.

Therefore, let us say that the technique, however we choose to label it, can easily be considered "omnipresent". That is, each "part" of the work seems to contain the "whole" of a technique which is multi-faceted and multi-focal. There is dialogue, prayer, history, Church tradition, faith and true-to -life miracles. At the same time, the "cast" of characters includes the Divine Holy Trinity above to the eternally condemned demons of hell below. Consequently, a ceaseless contrast between "lo terrenal" and "lo divino" creates undeniable *polarization.* Yet, the dominating force of the "holy other" or "lo más allá" *unifies* the work constantly. Also, a pervasive irony characterizes *La Mística Ciudad.* It is a "holy" irony, which at all times accompanies the sacred "personajes" of the work. For example, while certain "characters" may appear to be scorned and poverty-stricken in the eyes of the world, they are favored and apprised in the eyes of God.

"...a los ojos del mundo tan solos, como pobres, y humildes peregrinos, sin que nadie de los mortales los reputase... pero o admirables

45

sacramentos del altíssimo ocultos a los mortales los reputase... pero o admirables sacramentos del altíssimo ocultos a los sobervios e ina escrutables para la prudencia carnal!" (Segunda parte, Libro IV, Cap. IX)

We come to appreciate even more a subtle irony when we consider how: Nature rules as a power over man yet its power is held as a sceptre in the hand of the Child Jesus. Mary, the Virgin is "la esclava del Señor" yet Queen of the universe. Christ — "El Rey Divino" — "accepts" crucifixion amid criminals and out of love for his persecutors. Heaven comes to earth, in the narrative, yet, the author is "spiritually" lifted to heavenly heights to receive the revelations of which her work is composed. Eternity seems placed within the confines of time. The invisible creatures take on a "corporeal form" and the unimaginable is described in finest detail.

María de Agreda literally worships God alone with her every word. And, if she attributes worth to earthly creatures, it is only in proportion to their surrender to Him.

The human is nearly wedded to the divine by the constant appearance of heavenly citizens (angels in particular) whose tasks vary from protecting and defending, to praising, serving, guiding or comforting etc. Their numbers are limitless. Sacred Scripture runs like a fiber through the text; they bear the effect of yeast in dough. The Scriptures can be likened to lattices to which the story clings. Yet, at the same time it appears that the Scriptures do the "peering" through the lattices of the work's narrative structure.

Lastly, even if the Venerable Mother intentionally chose to narrate this "historia" (I do not belive she so "chose"), we must realize how risky an undertaking it actually was. Let us recall that her work was recorded in an age and historical period during which people were executed for the mere mention of such ideas!

Can we possibly cast this work aside as just another example of the conventional "good vs. evil" technique? Granted, I at first glance, we might consider María de Agreda's narrative technique and structure as both typically and perhaps even exclusively religious. Intrinsically, however, I re-emphasize that her narrative technique, in particular, is an ingenious reversal of the ordinary direction taken by literature. Namely, María de Agreda uses literature itself as a springboard or channel for religious (mystical) expression whereas historically or at least conventionally, religion was taken full advantage of as a vehicle for literary creation. Again, ultimate importance and interest dwell in the fact that the relation between her literary discourse here and the religious postures of her work strongly suggests an argument for a break with the concept that prose is only fiction.

No single attempt is sufficient to appropriately situate a work such as this, amid the "myriades" of already existing Spanish literary masterpieces. I hardly have as my goal any such aspiration. However, one can hope that we may begin to discover and appreciate "family ties" between *La Mística Ciudad* and Spain's phenomenal repertoire of prose literature. It is indeed far less painful to argue in favor of María de Agreda's literary contribution in this case than to defend her theological accuracy.

As a final note, I repeat: one field of study may choose to consider the work as offensive to the Church, or another, a behavioral deviance, yet another, some sort of social mishap. The literary critic, however, need only come to appreciate it as a contribution to Spanish Baroque literature. Let those who will scrutinize do so; let those who must analize do the same but let the lovers of true Spanish baroque literature at last discover and enjoy!

Works Cited and Consulted

Agreda, Sor María de Jesús de. *La Mística Ciudad de Dios*. Madrid: por Bernardo Villa Diego, 1670.

Alborg, Juan Luis. *Historia de la Literatura Española*. 4 vols. Madrid: Editorial Gredos, 1980.

Arintero, O.P., S.T.M., *The Mystical Evolution in the Development of the Church*. 2 Vols. St Louis: The Herder Book Co., 1951.

Arroyo, Ciriaco Moron. *La Mística Española*. Madrid: Ediciones Alcalá, S.A., 1971.

Artiles, Joaquin. *Los recursos literarios de Bercero*. Madrid: Editorial Gredos, 1968.

Bakhtin, Mikhail, *The Dialogical Principle* trans., Wlad Godzick, ed. Tzvetan Todorov, Minneapoli: Uuniversity of Minneapolis Press, 1984.

Bazán, Doña Emilia Pardo. *Obras Completas de Doña Emilia Pardo Bazán*. 3 vols., ed. H.L. Kirby, Jr. Madrid: Aguilar, 1973.

Bazán, Doña Emilia Pardo. *Vida de la Virgen María*. Barcelona: Montaner y Simon, 1899.

Biblioteca de Autores Españoles, tomo centisemonoveno. Real Academia Española 108 — Perfil Histórico de Sor María de Jesús de Agreda. 109 — Cartas de Sor María y Felipe IV.

Booth, Wayne, C. *The Rhetoric of Fiction*. Chicago: The University of Chicago Press, 1970.

Brown, Henry. *Darkness or light; an essay in the theory of divine contemplation*. St. Louis Mo.: Herder Press, 1925.

Brown, Huntington. *Prose Styles*. Minneapolis: The University of Minneapolis Press, 1966.

Brown, Raymond E. 5.5., Fitzmyer, John S.J., and Murphy, E., The Jerome Biblical Commentary. New Jersey: Prentice Hall Inc., 1968.

Bruggemann, Waltar. *Genesis: A Bible Commentary for Teaching*. Atlanta: John Knox Press, 1982.

Calderón, Correa E., Lazaro, Carreter F., *Como se comenta un texto literario*. Madrid: Ediciones Anaya, 1969.

Castro Américo. *La realidad histórica de España. edición renovada. México: Porrua, 1982*.

Chapman, Charles E. A History of Spain.. New York: The Macmillian Co., 1918.

Descola, Jean. *A History of Spain.*. New York: Knopf Press, 1963.

Dominguez Berruta Juan. *Filosofía mística española*. Instituto Luis Vives, 1947.

Dominguez, Ortiz, Antonio. *Historia de España, Alfaguara, El Antiguo régimen; los reyes Católicos y los austrias*. Alfaguara: Alianza universidad, 1974.

Eakin, John Paul. *Fictions in Autobiography: Studies in the Art of Self-Invention*. Princeton, N.J. : Princeton University Press, 1985.

Estrada, Lopez. *Historia y crítica de la literatura española*. 2 vols. Barcelona: Editorial Crítica, 1980.

Feder, Lillian. *Madness in Literature.*. Princeton, N.J. Princeton: University Press, 1980.

Ferrater Ora, Jose. *Diccionario de filosofía.*. 4th ed. Buenos Aires: Editorial Sudamericana, 1958.

Gariano, Carmelo. *Gonzalo de Bercero, 13th century.*. "Milagros de Nuestra Señora." Madrid: Editorial Gredos, 1965. Graef, Holda C. *Mystics of our times*. London: Borns and Oates, 1962.

Green, Otis H. *Spain and the Western Tradition.*. 4 vols. Madison, Milwaukee and London The University of Wisconsin Press, 1968.

Halloway, John. *Narrative and Structure*. New York: Cambridge University Press, 1979.

Hamilton, Earl. J. *The American treasure and the Prices of revolution in Spain, 1501-1650*. Harvard: Harvard Press, 1934.

Happold, F. Grossfield. *Mysticism: a study and an anthropology*. Baltimore: Penguin Press, 1967.

Hardon, John A., S.J. *Modern Catholic Dictionary.*. New York: Doubleday and Company., Inc., 1979.

Hatzfield, Helmut. *Estudios literarios sobre Mística española.*. Madrid: Editorial Gredos, second edition, 1968.

Heureux Aloysius Gonzaga, Mother. *The Mystical Vocabulary*. Washington: Catholic University Press, 1956.

Hubbard, Alice Philena. *Seven Spanish Mystics.*. Cambridge, Mass.: Society of St. John the Evangelist, 1947.

Inbert, Enrique Anderson. *¿Qué es la prosa?* Argentina: Editorial Columbia, 1963.

Karvin, Bruce, *The Mind of the Novel Reflexive Fiction and the Ineffable*. Princeton, N.J.: Princeton University Press, 1982.

Kendrick, Thomas. *Mary of Agreda. The life and legend of a Spanish nun.* Londres: Routelege and Kegan Paul, 1958.

Llorca, S. J., Bernadino. *Historia de la Igesia Católica.*. Madrid: Biblioteca de Autores Cristianos, 1950.

Mendieta, Gerónimo. *Historia eclesiástica indiana.*. Madrid: Linotipias Monserrat, 1973.

Menendez Pidal, Ramón. *Estudios Literarios.* Madrid: Espasa-Calpe, 1968.

Menendez Pidal, Ramón. *Historia de España.* Madrid: Espasa-Calpe, 1935.

Menendez Pidal, Ramón. *Historia de las Ideas Estéticos en año 1990.* ed. nacional. Madrid: Consejo superior de Investigaciones científicas, 1962.

Menendez y Pelayo, Marcelino. *Historia de la Literature Española desde las origines hasta el año 1900.* Madrid: La España Moderna, 1901.

Menendez y Pelayo, Marcelino. *Origines de la Novela.* Edición preparada por Enrique Sanchez Reyes. 2a edición. Madrid: Consejo superior de Investigaciones científicas, 1961.

Miller, J. Hillis. *Aspects of Narrative.* New York: Columbia University Press, 1971.

Monner Sans, Ricardo. "Ideas Politicas y morales de Sor María de Agreda.", Revista de la Universidad de Buenos Aires, segunda serie, sec, VI., 1926.

Montenegro Duque, Angel. *Historia de Espana.* Madrid: Gredos, 1972.

Morison, Fiscar. *What the Universities of Europe, the Religious orders and Learned Men say of the "Ciudad de Dios."* California: Academy Library Guild Press, 1914.

Morison, Fiscar. *Life of the Virgin.* 2 vols. Chicago: Theopolitan Press, 1914.

Molotinia, Toribio. *Historia de los indios de Nueva España.* Madrid: Castalia, 1985.

McKenzie, John L., S.J. *Dictionary of the Bible.* New York: Macmillian Publishing Co., Inc., 1975.

Olney, James. *Metaphors of self: the meaning of autobiobraphy.* Princeton N.J.: Princeton University Press, 1972.

Orsini, Mathieu. *Life of the Blessed Virgin Mary.* New York: Peter F. Collier pub., 1970.

Osborne, Robert E. *Emilia Párdo Bazán: Su vida y sus obras*. México: Colección Stadium, 1964.

Patrides, C.A. *Premises and Motifs in Renaissance thought and literature*. Princeton, N.J. : Princeton University Press, 1979.

Payne, Stanley G. *A History of Spain and Portugal*. 2 vols. Madison Wisconsin Press, 1973.

Peers, Edgar A., *Studies of the Spanish Mystics*. 2 vols. London: The Sheldon Press, 1927.

Peers E. Allison. *Studies of the Spanish Mystics*. New York: The Macmillian Co., 1951.

Pfandl, Ludwig. *Cultura y Costumbres del pueblo español de los siglos XVI y XVII*. Barcelona: Araluce, 1929.

Pond, Kathleen. *The Spirit of the Spanish Mystics*. New York: P.J. Kenedy and Sons, 1958.

Ricard, Roberto, *Estudios de literatura religiosa española*. Madrid: Editorial Gredos, 1964.

Santullano, Luis. *Místicos Españoles*. Madrid: Instituto escuela, 1934.

Segro, Cesare. *Structures and time: narration, poetry models*. Illinois: University of Chicago Press, 1979.

Simon, Raphael. *Hammer and Fire*. Mass.St. Bede's Publications, 1987.

Skinner, John D.D. *Critical and exegetical commentary on Genesis*. New York: Scribner's sons, 1969.

Telvier, Harold. *Animate Illusions*. Nebraska: University of Nebraska Press, 1974.

Uspensky, A.B. *A poetics of composition*. California University of California Press, 1973.

Vives, J, Vicens. *Historia Social y Económica de España y America*, 5 vol. España: Universidad de Barcelona, 1972.

Wardropper, Bruce. *Historia de la poesía a lo divino en la cristiandad occidental*. revista de Occidente, Madrid. 1958.

Wirt, Sherwood E. *The Confessions of Saint Augustine*. Michigan: Clarion Press, 1986.

Zuleta, Emilia. *Historia de la crítica española contemporanea*. Madrid: Gredos, 1974.

Appendix I

The following appendix includes chapter titles taken from Part II, books 3, 4, 5, 6, 7 and 8 of Sor María de Jesús de Agreda's *La Mística Ciudad de Dios*. These titles are from the 1670 Spanish version of the text. The purpose of this appendix is to illustrate the unusual and extensive details found in Sor María's writing. Such detail far surpasses any information available in Sacred Scripture.

Tabla
De Los Capitulos
Que Contiene
Esta Segunda Parte
Libro Tecero
Tercera Parte Capitulo Primero

cución de la Encarnación, y Redención humana, y concede su Magestad la petición, fol. 43

Libro Quarto, Tercera Parte

el Nacimiento de nuestro Salvador, y los Pastores vinieron a adorarle, fol. 229.

Libro Quinto, Tercera Parte

Libro Sexto, Tercera Parte

comunión para su tiempo, y síguele a Gerusalén con la Madalena, y otras santas mugeres, fol. 66.

Cap. X. Celebra Christo nuestro Salvador la última Cena Legal con sus Discipulos, y lavales los pies. Tiene su Madre Santissima inteligencia, y noticia de todos estos Mysterios, fol. 73.

Cap. XI. Celebra Christo nuestro salvador Sento sacramental, consagrando en la Eucaristía su sagrado, y verdadero cuerpo, y sangre, las oraciones, y peticiones que hizo: comulgo a su Madre Santíssima, y otros Mysterios que sucedieron en esta ocasión, fol. 85.

Cap. XII. La oración que hizo nuestro Salvador en el Huerto, y sus Mysterios, y lo que de todos conoció su Madre Santíssima, fol. 98.

Cap. XIII. La Entrega, y Prendimiento de nuestro salvador, por la trayción de Judas, y lo que en esta ocasión hizo María Santíssima, y algunos Mysterios deste passo, fol. 109.

Cap. XIV. La fuga, y división de los Apostoles, con la Prisión de su Maestro; la noticia que tuvo su Madre Santíssima, y lo que hizo en esta ocasión; la condenación de Judas, y turbación de los Demonios, con lo que iban conociendo, fol. 119.

Cap. XV. Llevan a nuestro salvador Jesús atado, y Preso a casa del Pontífice Anas; lo que sucedió en este passo, y lo que padeció en el su Beatíssima Madre, fol. 129.

Cap. XVI. Fue llevado Christo nuestro salvador a casa de el Pontífice Cayfas, donde fue acusado, y preguntado, si era Hijo de Dios, y San Pedro le negó otras dos vezes; lo que María Santíssima hizo en este passo, y otros Mysterios ocultos, fol. 136.

Cap. XVII. Lo que padeció nuestro salvador Jesús, después de la negación de San Pedro, hasta la mañana; y el dolor grande de su Madre Santíssima, fol. 145.

Cap. XVIII. Júntase el Concilio Viérnes por la mañana, para substanciar la causa contra nuestro Salvador Jesus. Remítenle a Pilatos, y sale al encuentro María Santíssima con San Juan Evangelista, y las tres Marías, fol. 152.

Cap. XIX. Remite Pilatos a Herodes la causa, y Persona de nuestro Salvador Iesús; acúsanle ante Herodes, y el le desprecia, y embia a Pilatos; síguele María Santissima, y lo que en este passo sucedió, fol. 162.

Cap. XX. Por mandado de Pilatos; fue acotado nuestro salvador Jesús, coronado de Espinas, y escarnecido, y lo que en este passo hizo María Santíssima, fol. 173.

Cap. XXI. Pronuncia Pilatos la sentencia de muerte contra el Autor de la Vida; lleva su Magestad la Cruz acuestas, en que ha de morir; siguele su Madre Santíssima, y lo que hizo la gran señora en este passo contra el Demonio, y otros sucessos, fol. 184.

Libro Septimo, Tercera Parte

seguir a la Iglesia, y lo que contra este enemigo hizo, amparando, y desendiendo a los Fieles. fol. 84.

Libro Ocho, Tercera Parte

Cap. 4. Destruye María Santíssima el Templo de Diana en Ephesso, llévanla sus Angeles al Cielo Impíreo, donde el Señor la prepara para entrar en batalla con el Dragon infernal, y vencele; comienza este Duelo por tentaciones de sobervia. fol. 231.

Cap. 5. Buelve de Ephesso a Jerusalén María Santíssima, llamada del Apóstol San Pedro, continúase la batalla con los Demonios, padece gran tormeta en el mar, y declaranse otros secretos sucedieron en ello. fol. 243.

Cap. 6. Vision María Santíssima los Sagrados Lugares, gana mysteriosos triunfos de los Demonios, vio en el Cielo la Divinidad con visión Beatífica celebran Concilio los Apóstoles, y los secreto ocultos que sucedieron en todo esto. fol. 255.

Cap. 7. Concluyó María Santíssima las batallas triunfando gloriosamente de los Demonios, como lo contiene S. Iuan en el cap. 12. de su Apocalipsi. fol 266.

Cap. 8. Declárase el Estado en que puso Dios a su madre Santíssima con visión de la Divinidad abstractiva, pero continua después que venció a lo Demonios, y el modo de obrar que en el tenía. fol. 179.

Cap. 9. El principio que tuvieron los Evangelistas y sus Evangelios, y lo que en esto hizo María Santíssima, aparecióse a S. Pedro en Antioquia, y en Roma, y otros favores Semejantes con otros Apóstoles. fol. 289.

Cap. 10. La memoria, y Exercicios de la Passión tenía María Santíssima, y la veneración con que recevia la Sagrada Comunión, y otras obras de vida perfectíssima. fol. 298.

Cap. 11. Levantó el Señor con nuevos beneficios María Santíssima sobre, el Estado que se dixó arriba en el cap. 8. deste libro. fol. 307.

Cap. 12. Como celebraba María Santíssima su Immaculada Concep-

62

ción, y Natividad, y los beneficios que estos días recibía de su Hijo Nuestro Salvador Jesús. fol. 314.

Cap. 13. Celebra María Santíssima otros beneficios y fiestas con sus Angeles, en especial su Presentación, y las festividades de S. Joachín, Santa Ana, y San Joseph. fol. 320.

Cap. 14. El admirable modo con que María Santíssima...

Cap. 16. Como celebraba María Santíssima las fiestas de la Ascensión de Christo Nuestro Salvador, y Venida de el Espíritu Santo, de los Angeles y Santos, y otra memorias de sus proprios beneficios. fol. 346.

Cap. 17. La Embaxada del Altíssimo que tuvo María Santíssima por el Angel San Gabriel de que le restaban tres años de vida, y lo que sucedió con este aviso del Cielo, a San Juan, y a todas las criaturas de la naturaleza. fol. 354.

Cap. 18. Como crecieron en los últimos días de María Santíssima los vuelos, y deseos de ver a Dios, despídese de los Lugares Santos, y de la Iglesia Católica, ordena su Testamento, assistiéndola la Santíssima Trinidad. fol. 362.

Cap. 19. El Tránsito felicíssimo, y glorioso de María Santíssima, y como los Apóstoles, y Discípulos llegaron antes a Ierusalén, y se hicieron presentes a el. fol. 371.

Cap. 20. Del Entierro de el Sagrado Cuerpo de María Santíssima, y lo que en el sucedió. fol. 378.

Cap. 21. Envió en el Cielo Empíreo la Alma de María Santíssima, y a imitación de Christo Nuestro Redemptor bolivió a resucitaria Sagrado Cuerpo, y en el subió otra vez a la Diestra del mismo Señor al tercero día. fol. 384.

Cap. 22. Fue Coronada María Santíssima por Reyna de los Cielos, y de todas las criaturas, confirmándola grandes privilegios en beneficio de los hombres. fol. 391.

Cap. 23. Confessión de Alavanza, y hazimiento de gracias, que yo la menor de los mortales Sor María de Jesús hizo al Señor, y a su Madre Santíssima por aver escrito esta Divina historia con el Magisterio de la misma Señora, y Reyna de el Cielo. fol. 397.

Protestación pública, petición, y concordia de este Convento, y Monjas Descalzas de la Immaculada Concepción de esta Villa de Agreda, para introducir por sus Patronos, y Protectores en primir lugar a la Soberana Reyna, y Señora del Cielo, y tierra, María Santíssima, y con su beneplácito al glorioso Principe San Miguel, y N. P. San Francisco. fol. 409.

Appendix II

This appendix traces in part the scrutiny of Sor Maria's work by church authorities. The "Censuras" contained within are also taken from the 1670 Spanish version of *La Mística Ciudad de Dios*. The purpose of Appendix II is to help illustrate the controversy and the polemics occasioned by her work.

Censura De La Obra, Comission, Y Licencia De Su Impression, Por La Religion De San Francisco

Fray Alonso Sallzanes, Ministro General, y siervo de toda la Orden de nuestro Seráfico Padre San Francisco, & c. Al R. P. Fr. Ioseph Ximénez Samaniego, Lector Iubilado, Ex-Prouincial, y Padre de nuestra Provincia de Burgos de la Regular Observancia de nuestro Seráfico Padre San Francisco, salud, y paz en nuestro Señor Iesu Christo.

Aviendo sido nuestro Seráfico Padre llamado por el Señor a la institu ción de su Religion Sagrada, para servicio de la Santa Iglesia, y utilidad Espiritual de los Fieles, es obligación de quien sucede a tan gran patriarca en el gobierno, y Prelacia General de su dilatada Familia, procurar por los medios convenientes, que los beneficios, que la Divina Providencia dispuso comunicar a los hijos de essa Santa Católica Iglesia, tomando por instrumento algún sujeto de los que militan debaxo de el gobierno desta Religión, no se escondan en los cerrados canceles de el silencio, sino, que se coloquen en el Candelero de la publicidad, para que iluminen a todos los que están en essa casa de Dios. En el segundo año de nuestro gobierno (no sin especial disposición Divina, como nos obliga a pensar lo inopinado de el sucesso, lo extraviado del viaje para el lugar, donde se enderecaba nuestro camino, el impulso interior que tubimos para hazerlo, y el consuelo espiritual que después sentimos nos hallamos en la Villa de Agreda, a tiempo, que la Venerable Madre Sor María de Jesús, Religiosa professa del Orden de la In- maculada Concepción de la Madre de Dios, y Abadesa de el Convento de

Descalcas de la misma Orde, sito extramuros de la dicha Villa, y sujeto a nuestra obediencia en nuestra Provincia de Burgos, persona, que por muchos años avia florecido con fama grande, y invariada de santidad, estaba en el aprieto de su enfermedad última; y aviedo assistido personalmete a su cabecera asta su dichosa muerte, que correspondió a la opinión de su vida, y celebrado los oficios funerales, procurado, que de la devoción fervorosa del Pueblo no se originasse contravenció alguna a los Breves Apostolicos, fuimos informados, que la dicha V. Madre dexaba algunos escritos de grande edificación, y doctrina, a que la avia obligado la Obediecia de sus Confessores, y Prelados. Recogímoslos conforme al debito de nuestra obligación, y lo principal que entre ellos hallamos, fue la Historia de la vida de la Madre de Dios, con este título: Mystica Ciudad de Dios, milagro de su Omnipotencia, y abismo de la gracia: Historia Divina, y vida de la Virgen Madre de Dios, Reyna, y Señora nuestra María Santíssima, restauradora de la culpa d Eua, y medianera de la gracia: manifestada en estos ultimos siglos por la misma Señora a su Esclava Sor María de Jesús, para nueva luz del mundo, alegría de la Iglesia Católica, y confianza de los mortales. Dividida en tres partes, y escrita en ocho libros, todos de la letra, y mano de la misma sierva de Dios, como se nos hizo evidente de la conferencia de ellos con otros escritos, y cartas notoriamente de su letra, y mano. Y aviendo leído parte desta obra, no sin grande admiración, y moción de nuestro interior, y conferido la materia con personas doctas, y espirituales de satisfacción entera, nos pareció sería de gran servicio de Dios, y utilidad de sus Fieles, que saliesse a luz luego, conforme a la facultad que dió el Señor Papa Vrbano VIII. practicada frequentemente en estos tiempos, si después de examinado con toda diligencia, se hallasse corresponder toda la obra sin dissonancia alguna, a lo que promete su título; y que era de nuestra obligación acudir con todo cuidado a este examen por los medios proporcionados a nuestra facultad.

Para cumplir con ella instituimos en este nuestro Convento de San Francisco de Madrid una Iunta particular de sujetos doctos, y experimentados en materias de espíritu, de diversas Provincias, de los mas graves, y calificados de esta Familia; estos fueron el Rmo. P. Fr. Iuan de Muniessa, Lector de Theologia, Calificador de el Santo oficio, Predicador de la Magestad Católica, después de Confessor de la Descalcas Reales de esta Corte, Provincial de nuestra Provincia de Aragon, Difinidor General, y Comissario General de esta Familia Cismontana, actual Padre de la Orden: El Rmo.P. Fr. Andrés de Guadalupe, Lector Iubilado, Ex-Prouincial, de nuestra Provincia de los Angeles, Vice-Comissario General de esta Familia, Confessor de las Sereníssimas Infantas de España, y actual Comissario General de las Indias: El Reverendo P. Fr. Iuan de Molino, Lector Iubilado, Calificador del Santo Oficio, Ex-Prouincial de nuestra Provincia de la Concepción, y Confessor de la Augustíssima Señora Emperatriz: El P. Fr. Christobal Delgadillo, Lector Iubilado, después de Confessor de las Descalcas Reales, y Custodio de nuestra Provincia de Castilla, actual Guardián de este nuestro Convento de S. Francisco de Madrid: El P. Fr. Bartolomé García de Escañuela, Lector Iubilado, Predicador de su Magestad, y Padre de nuestra Provincia de Granada: El P. Fr. Andrés de Fuentemayor, Difinidor de nuestra Provincia de Burgos, que fue por muchos años Confessor de la misma Venerable Madre, y con quien ella comunicó las cosas de su espíritu asta la hora de su muerte: y aviendo señalado horas competentes en nuestra presencia, con assistencia de todos los referidos Padres, se fue leyendo la referida obra, desde el principio al fin, sin dexar sentencia, que no se examinasse, ni aún término en que no se hiziesse atento reparo; y después de este examen, en que se gastaron algunos meses, todos unánimes fuimos de parecer, que en la sobredicha Historia, ninguna cosa se contenía disonancia a la Fe, o buenas costumbres, antes bien todo lo que enseñaba era conforme a las doctrinas Católicas, y que por ninguna de las Reglas, que dan los Mysticos para discernir las Revelaciones verdaderas de las falsas, se podía entrar en sospecha de las que componen esta Historia, sino, que conforme a essas Reglas se podía hazer juizio probable por via de doctrina de que eran verdaderamente divinas; y que assí, atenta la utílissima enseñanza, que en toda la obra parecía notoria, sería de grande servicio a Dios, gloria de María Santíssima, y provecho de los Fieles, saliesse a la luz pública para edificación común. Mas porque el Demonio, que como cruel enemigo siempre reputa por daño proprio nuestro bien, suele valiéndose de diversos pretextos de zelo, o de piedad, pretender con todo esfuerzo embarazar las obras de que teme tanto detrimento; pareció a la Junta se previniesse su invasión, haziendo Notas a los lugares, que pareciessen más difíciles: y permitiendo a la obra las doctrinas generales, que conducen a formar rectamente el juizio común de ella.

Conforme à este parecer determínamos se tratasse de la impressión desta Historia, y aviéndose de encargar este trabajo, según lo resuelto, a persona de entera satisfacción, Nos, teniéndola de la doctrina, piedad, y providencia de V. P. por el temor de las presentes le ordenamos, y a mayor mérito se lo mandamos por Santa obediencia, que tome este negocio a su cuenta, con el cuydado, que pide su gravedad, haziendo las Notas, y prefaciones, que la parecieren necessarias, conforme al parecer de la dicha Junta arriba referido, y exornando la edición con todo lo que le pareciere conveniente; con tal, que en ninguna cosa, por leve que sea, varie, añada, ni

67

dísminuya el Texto que escribió la dicha Venerable Madre; que para esso entregamos a V. P. con esta un traslado de dicha obra, conferido, y ajustado en nuestra presencia por la referida Iunta, con el mismo original escrito, como dicho es, de mano, y letra de la misma Sierva de Dios; y mandamos a V. P. por la misma obediencia, presida a la impressión, cuidando se haga con toda legalidad por el exemplar que lo entregamos, sin variación alguna; y si por descuido de los Impressores, o Corrector se cometiere algún yerro, V. P. lo note, y haga se corrija en la se de erratas, de suerte, que en nada (quanto possible fuere) se falte a la verdad que pide la materia. Y esta nuestra patente sirva de Aprobación, y Licencia quanto de parte de la Religión se requiere, para hazer la impressión de dicha Historia, y con la diligencia referida, examinada, y por concorde parecer de Varones tan eruditos, y piadosos aprobada, con cuyo juyzio nos conformamos. Pero las Notas, y prefaciones, que V. P. trabajare, no las imprimirá sin traerlas primero a Vos, para que examinadas por nuestro orden, y hallándose (como esperamos) dignas de aprobación, le concedamos licencia especial para hazerlo: De catero servatis servandis. Dada en el dicho nuestro Convento de San Francisco de Madrid, firmada de nuestra mano, sellada con el sello mayor de nuestro oficio, y refrendada de nuestro Secretario en doce de Noviembre de mil y seiscientos y sesenta y ocho años.

Fray Alonso Salizanes,

Ministro General

Por mandado de su Reverendíssima,

Fray Patricio Tyrelo,

Secretario General de la Orden

Censura Del Reverendissimo Padre Maestro Andres Mendo, de la Compañía de Iesus, Predicador de su Magestad, Calificador del Consejo de la Inquisición suprema, Lector que fue de Theologia, y Escritura en Salamanca, Y Examinador Synodal de su Obispado.

Por comissión del Señor Doctor D. Francisco Forteza, Vicario de esta Villa de Madrid, e vistro, leído, y examinado con grandíssima atención las tres partes de la Mystica Ciudad de Dios, Historia Divina, y vida de María Reyna, y Señora nuestra, que dexó escritas, y perfectamente dispuestas la Venerable Madre Sor María de Jesús, Religiosa, y Abadesa de el Convento de la Inmaculada Concepción de la Villa de Agreda. Lectura a sido, que me a causado tantas admiraciones, como renglones tiene, Mas e aprendido de ella, que de quantos libros en muchos años con desuelo continuo, e estudiado, en todas las materias que toca; por la claridad, destreza, y profundidad con que habla. La propriedad en los términos, la puntualidad en las locuciones, el acierto en las más utiles dificultades, motivan a una veneración, y pasmo. Bien se reconoce, que es doctrina del Cielo, y que guió la pluma superior mano. Si es toda esta obra luzes para el entendimiento, que le ilustran, no es menos llamas para la voluntad, que la inflaman;

69

espolean a la mayor tibieza, y afervorizan a la virtud mas crecida. Con leer este libro atentamente, saldrá uno docto; con leerle exactamente, se moverá a ser Santo; porque sus documentos auyentan ignorancias, y excitan a obrar acciones heroycas: Esta es una mina preciosa, que se a descubierto, para enriquezer a la Iglesia, de la qual sacarán todos los estados los metales, y piedras de mas valor, para aliñar, y componer sus almas, y potencias.

Estrañará alguno dos cosas. La primera, el que una muger aya escrito obra tan consumada; pués en ella usa de toda la Escritura con raras noticias; interpreta con novedad muchos lugares de ella, sin que asta aora los Santos Padres, y los Interpretes ayan dado tan singulares exposiciones; traduce con palabras adequadas a nuestra lengua las clausulas, y periodos de las Divinas Letras, y declara los sentidos mas arduos. En las materias, que la Theologia Escólastica disputa, es admirable su comprehensión, y delgadeza; y en estilo terso, y claro explica lo que gasta muchos argumentos, y discursos; via de términos tan ajustados, como si ubiera cursado las Escuelas. No se desliza a temeridad, o ignoracia, tratando los puntos mas dificiles, sutiles, y escabrosos; y en su doctrina puede aprender, el que mas ubiere estudiado. En la ciencia Mystica, desde el principio al sin son estos escritos un assombro; no ay delicadeza de espíritu, que no quede de nuevo ilustrado; ni grados de persección, en que no de altíssimos documentos. Los caminos para adquirir virtudes para hallar a Dios para seguirle por la via purgativa, iluminativa, y unitiva, se allarán con celestial doctrina. Las astucias, y tentaciones de el Demonio, se descubren: los auxilios Divinos se proponen: los modos de vencer a los enemigos invisibles, y a nuestras passiones, se enseñan y las alturas de la contemplación se pone a la vista. No es fácil, que la cortedad de mis vozes diseñe algo de la grandeza de esta obra; y por esso dixe, que acaso alguno estrañarla, que una muger fuesse su Autora.

Pero leyendo el Prólogo, y Introducción cada una de las tres partes de esta Historia, quedará satisfecho, quien hiziere el reparo, viendo, que le hizo con grande eficazia la misma que la escribió, y que no pudo resistirse a preceptos de sus Prelados, y Confessores, y a otros mas superiores de Dios, y de la Sacratíssima Virgen. No pudiera por sí sola la Venerable Sor María de Jesús alcanzar tan profundos, y escondidos Mysterios; pero que mucho los alcanzasse, si iba enseñándoselos Maria Señora nuestra, y como llevándola la mano para escribirlos sus Angeles! Aquel Señor, que es en sus Santos admirable, que haze discretas, y eloquetes las lenguas de los Infantes, y de su boca recibe con gusto las alabanzas, quiso, que las de su puríssima Madre se pronunciassen por boca de una muger, y se escribiessen con su pluma; para que las acciones todas de la vida de la Reyna do los Cielos, ignoradas en gran parte, aora se manifestassen al mundo y se aumentas se su devoción en los Fieles con que tubiessen una prenda grande de su salvación. No puede nuestra limitad capacidad comprehender el abismo de la Sabiduría de Dios y lo investigable de sus consejos y as sí es en vano discurrir, porque dilato dar estas noticias asta los presentes siglos; aunque la misma Sierva de Dios da las razones de esta dilación.

En los passados ubo mugeres de insigne santidad, y sabiduría, y sin tocar en Santa Catalina, que confundió a los más Sabios Filósofos Gentiles con su ciencia ni en Santa Brigida, que escribió sus revelaciones de que la Iglesia haze memoria en la creación que la señala; ni en otras muchas, cuyos escritos veneramos; en este último siglo Santa Teresa de Jesús prodigio de Santidad, honra de España, escribió los libros, que la misma Iglesia en su oración llama doctrina Celestial; y quien los lee, se admira, de que en una muger cupiesse tan relevante sabiduría, Aun en tiempo más cercano escribió la Venerable Doña Marina de Escobar la doctrina, y revelaciones, que se contienen en la primera parte de la Historia de su vida, tan leyda de todos, y admirada, y las que en la segunda parte saldrán a la luz pública. Pues no estando la mano de Dios abreviada, no a de motivar estrañez el que se escribiesse toda esta obra, y se dispusiesse cabalmente por una muger, que sobre ser de tan realizadas virtudes y tan favorecida de la Magestad Divina, y de su Madre Puríssima, fue de rara capacidad, prendas, y entendimiento, de que tantos son testigos; y no es flaca prueba, el averla elegido con dispensación de veinte y cinco años de edad por Abadesa de su Convento, continuando toda su vida el mismo oficio con suma aprobación de sus Preldos, y de sus Súbditas.

La segunda cosa, que también alguno podría estrañar, es, el referirse en esta Historia puntos inauditos de que no avía conocimiento, acciones de la Virgen no sabidas: favores, y privilegios ignorados raros y singulares casos y sucessos de su vida; que ni escribieron los evangelistas, ni entre ellos San Iuan que la asistió siempre, y veneró como a Madre, sin apartase de su compañia, ni los tocaron, ni conocieron después los Doctores, y Padres de la Iglesia, ni otros interpretes, que han escrito tanto de María Señora nuestra; pues en ninguno se hallarán muchíssimas cosas especiales, que se contienen en esta obra.

Pero ya previno esta dificultad la misma Venerable Madre Sor María de Jesús, y aun la adelanta, llegando a discurrir, que se juzgarían sus revelaciones por consideraciones pías, meditadas en la oración, o ajustadas a la verosimilitud. Quitóla nuestro Señor su rezelo, y con los preceptos humanos, y divinos, que tubo, fue escribiéndo, y dio razones, y motivos,

71

porque avían estado ocultos tantos sucessos, y porque no los avían escrito los Historiadores Sagrados. Le se lo que dize, y cesará el reparo de la novedad. Para que yo aya assentido, a que passó assí todo lo que refiere, no e necesitado de otro motivo, que de leerlo, y me persuado, sucederá a los demás lo mismo. Porque ni la idea humana bassa adelinear los sucessos; ni el discurso a formar tan admirable armonía: ni la meditación devota a eslabonar tan preciosa cadena El lo esta publicando superior mano, y que el dedo de Dios apuntaba verdades tan recónditas. La admiración que se concibe leyéndolo: la suavidad, y dulzura, que causa en el alma; los afectos fervorosos, que en el corazón engendra, efectos son de ser todas las cláusulas dictadas por María Señora nuestra. Y si yo con mi tibieza lo e experimentado, estándolo leyéndo, que sentirán, y experimentarán otros? En persuadirse a que son ciertas las grandezas, prerogativas, y privilegios, que se quentan de la Santíssima Virgen, nadie tendrá que escrupulizar, pues todo cabe en quien fue Madre de Dios; y los Interpretes, y Autores muy comunmente enseñan que emos de atribuirla las persecciones, y excelencias todas, que no son repugnantes, y fueren proporcionadas a la dignidad, a que la encurmbró la Magestad Divina. Y quanto en esta Historia se pone, es muy proporcionado a essa dignidad, sin que embuelva repugnancia.

Entre otros frutos, que se cogeran desta obra, sera muy gustoso para la devoción entrañada en los corazones, ver manifestada la Inmaculada Concepción de María Señora nuestra sin pecado original en el primer insantante de su ser natural, que se propone en muchos lugares desta Historia: en especial desde el Capítulo quince del Libro primero de la primera parte; y aun sin el debito de contraer esse pecado: como consta del Capítulo quarto antecedente; y uno, y otro ensañado por la misma Virgen haze mas cierto, y firme, lo que ya nadie contradice. Las vozes termino, y razones con que se declara este mysterio, captan la atención, convencen el entendimiento; y no dexan sombra de dudar al discurso.

El crédito mayor del acierto destos libros son ellos mismos. Mas no es pequeña confirmación el aver sido tan examinado, y aprobado el espíritu de la Venerable Sor María de Jesús, que los escribió: pues como desde sus principios fue tan levantada, puso singular cuydado la Sagrada Religión de S. Francisco, de governarle con gran destreza, y vigilancia, y de poner Confessores doctíssimos, y espirituales que le rigiessen; dos de ellos conocí yo, y comuniqué, que fueron el Reverendíssimo Fr. Francisco Andrea de la Toree, y el Reverendíssimo Fray Miguel Gutierrez, Provinciales que fueron ambos de la Provincia de Burgos; Varones llanamente Sabios en toda Theologia, Escolástica, Moral, y Mystica. Y el que estos, y otros semejantes después de largo examen, y comunicación constantemente aprobassen el tenor de vida de esta Sierva de Dios, sus acciones, sus virtudes, sus revelaciones, y escritos, remirando en el los asta los puntos y comas prueba grande es de que en ellos son todas sinceras verdades, sin mezcla de revelaciones apocrisas, ni de discursos vanos, pues no tiraba linea, que no la registrasse, y diesse razón de ella una, y otra vez a sus Confessores, y prelados, que ni la solicitaban aplausos, ni mostraban convivencia, ni permitían exterioridades. Assí reconocido bien la prudencia con que se a procedido, pués estando acabada esta obra el año de sesenta, no se a tratado de dar a la estampa asta aora, después de aver muerto la Venerable Sor María; y de averla revisto, y examinado con muchos ojos y con increibles desvelos.

Y para que en vida, y muerte tubiesse cabal aprobación el espíritu desta Sierva de Dios con especial providencia suya, assistió a su muerte el Reverendíssimo Padre Maestro, Fr. Alonso Salizanes Ministro General de la Orden de S. Francisco (cuya sabiduría, y prendas son dignísimas del puesto que ocupa) para que como cabeza de toda la Religión dieuse el más auténtico testimonio de la rara obediencia profunda humildad, insigne paciencia, y de las demas virtudes cuyos efectos vio aquellos últimos días, reconociendo la margarita inestimable, que estaba escondida en la concha a aquel cuerpo mortal, y aprobando el concepto común, que todos avían echo de su santidad heroyca Y dispuso también nuestro Señor esta assistencia, para que recogiendo sus papeles, y entre ellos esta Historia, solicitasse el que volvien dose a repetir el examen della, salga a la luz pública, que es el mas estimable beneficio, que podía hazer a domésticos, y estraños.

Grande apoyo es también de la seguridad del espíritu, y de los escritos de esta Sierva de Dios, el aver tenido con ella por muy largo tiempo frequente comunicación por cartas el Señor Felipe cuarto nuestro Rey (que este en gloria) en que trataría negocios de suma monta, y fiaría de sus respuestas la luz para el acierto, y de sus oraciones las dichas para su alma, y para las empressas arduas, que encomendasse a ellas. Pues un Monarcha tan piadoso, tan circunspecto, y tan prudente no ubiera comencado, y continuado esta comunicación con cartas escritas de su propria mano, sin aver primero inquirido, examinado, y sabido con toda moral certeza, quan seguro era el espíritu de la Venerable Sor Marí a, y quanto obraba Dios en ella, participándola sus luzes, gracias, dones, y sabiduría.

Bien puede la esclarecida Seráfica religión del gran Patriarca S. Francisco gloriarse de tener tal Hija, y aunque muchas suyas amontonaron riquezas espirituales, no se si se puede dezir, que esta las excedió a todas; por lo menos no será fácil el hallar en otra ventajas. Millares de Escritores en todas ciencias, y facultades a tenido, con que a ilustrado la Iglesia, adelantado las Escuelas, desterrado ignorancias, y convencido heregias; quente desde oy un millar mas, pues esta Escritora vale por mil. Aquel Divino Padre de familias, que (como ella misma dize en el discurso desta Historia) saca de su inagotable tesoro Mysterios antiquos, y nuevos, a querido manifestar aora tantos nuevos no por nuevamente sucedidos sino por ocultos, y retirados asta este tiempo por altíssimo fines de su Divina providencia, y que la pluma de una muger varonil los escriba, añadiendo la doctrina, que la Virgen Santíssima la enseñaba, sobre cada capítulo, que escribía, Admirémos las obras de Dios, y engrandezcámosle por los beneficios, y favores, que no cesa de hazer al mundo, y a la Iglesia por medio de almas tan puras. Los que hizo a esta Sierva de Dios, fuera, delos contenidos en estaHistoria, y las virtudes, que exercitó en Heroyco grado, no es bien, que esten en silencio, con que el deseo público será, de que se escriba, y estampe su vida, la qual hará maravillosa consonancia, armonía, y correspondencia con esta Historia; pues se afiancará el conocimiento, de que escribió con acierto, firmeza, y seguridad, la que vivió con tantos colmos de santidad, y levantada virtud.

No parezcan para una censura escusados, y prolixos estos preámbulos; que para daría en materias tan altas, tan delgadas, y por la mayor parte nuevas an sido fundamentos sorcosos. Y sobre ellos diré mi sentir, ni usando de aprobaciones panegyricas, como suelen darse a otras obras, sino de rixida censura, en que me sugeto a la corrección de la Iglesia Cathólica, y no doy a las revelaciones contenidas en esta Historia mas certeza, y credibilidad, que la que permiten los Decretos de la Santidad de Urbano VIII. los quales protesto, que guardo. Iuzgo, pues, que este libro que se divide en tres partes, de la Mystica Ciudad de Dios, Historia de la vida de María Señora nuestra, en todas ellas no contiene doctrina, successo, cláusula, razón, ni palabra, que se oponga a la Sagrada Escritura, ni a la Fe Católica, ni a la piedad, ni buenas costumbres. Y que todas están llenas de superiores, y sanos documentos; mueven a alabanzas de nuestro gran Dios: a devoción con su Santíssima Madre: a salir de culpas: a adquirir virtudes, y anhelar a la cumbre de la perfección. Con que para el provecho de todos, y bien común de las almas, se puede, y es debido dar licencia para que se impriman, y solicitar, que sea sin ninguna tardanza, porque no se carezca de los grandes bienes que espero an de seguirse de leer esta Celestial Historia. En este Colegio Imperial de la Compañia de Jesús de Madrid, a 29, de Octubre de l666.

Andrés Mendo,

74

Licencia De El Ordinario.

Vista la Censura, y Aprobación arriba puesta, damos licencia por lo que a Nos toca para que se impriman estos libros en ella referidos. Madrid, y Noviembre, seis de mil y seiscientos y sesenta y seis años.

Hector D. Francisco Forteza,

Por su mandado.

Juan de Ribera Muñuz

Censura, Y Aprobación De El Rmo Padre, y Ilustríssimo Señor D. Fr. Diego de Silva, Maestro en Sagrada Theologia, después de General de la Orden de el gran Patriarca de las Religiones San Benito, aora Obispo de Guadix.

Por comisión de V A. e visto los tres cuerpos de Historia de la Mystica Ciudad de Dios milagro de su Omnipotencia, y abismo de la gracia, Historia Divina, y vida de la Virgen Santíssima Madre de Dios, Reyna, y Señora nuestra, restauradora, y medianera de la gracia. Escrita en este siglo por su devota Sor María de Jesús, Abadesa de el Convento de la Inmaculada Concepción de la Villa de Agreda, manifestada por la Virgen Santíssima para nueva luz de el mundo, alegría de la Iglesia Católica, y confianza de los mortales; y aunque V. A. la sugeto a la Censura, ella nació para la admiración; todo es Divino quanto contiene, y de los tesoros de la Divinidad haze ostentación feliz de la Sabiduría eterna encarnada y abundante en la vida prodigiosa de la Madre de Dios, la novedad de las riquezas Celestiales que manifiesta, son rayos de la Omnipotencia, que penetran los corazones humanos y los abraza en la llama de el amor Divino, no se a manifestado a los mortales Caracteres de tanta erudición, tanto provecho, tanta novedad: no solo es digna esta obra de ver la luz, sino executad porque salga a darla a todos los hombres. Con Rayos de Sol en lugar de lineas avía de escribirse esta doctrina tan sutil, y felíz en lo escolástico, que dibuxa; tan soberana en el estilo, con que la declara; tan provechosa en el fruto, que deduce; tan gloriosa en los documentos, que repite; y tan advertida en todas las Theologias, que assegura, escolástica, expositia, y mystica. Lo suma desta Sabiduría no pide alabanza, sino admiración: Prolixa lans est que non queritar, sed tenetur; dixo San Ambrosio en menos empeño Pues ninguna puede igualar al assumpto de la obra, que es la vida de María Santíssima. Muy a la letra le ajusta este assumpto la parábola del Evangelio de San Matheo, cap. 13. donde dize: Simile estregnum Caelorum Thesauro abscondito in agro, quem qui innenit bomo abscondit, o pre gaudio illius vadit, o vendit universo, que babet, o emit agrum illum. Reyno de los Cielos es este trabajo, porque esta coronado de tantas estrellas de erudición, de tantos rayos de Divinidad, que ninguna tiene de la semejanza del Cielo tanta propriedad. Tesoro es el más copioso de la Sabiduría eterna, escondido hasta estos siglos, manifestado para nuestra riqueza. Hallóle la Sierva de Dios; arcaduz por donde el mismo Dios nos comunicó las aguas mas puras que derramó la fuente del Parayso en la Católica Iglesia. Correno para que se buelva a esconder, sino para que riegue el campo esteril, y seco de la Christiandad. Hallóle una Sierva de Dios en el retiro de su Convento de la Inmaculada Concepción de la Villa de Agreda, y aunque por su grande humildad pretendió esconderle o no escribirle, o después de escrito quemarle, pero bolvió por su causa el tesorero, y nuestra gran necessidad nos le grangeo por dispensación misericordiosa, y Divina. Vendió todo su caudal la Autora de estos volumenes para comprar el tesoro, y este aunque parece vendido se da de valde a la Iglesia: Venite, emite absque argento. Porque ni ay riquezas, ni méritos para comprar tanta felicidad. No tiene precio, ni conmutación margarita tan preciosa. Todo quanto se escribiere, es menos. Todo lo que se a manifestado, no iguala. Venderse todo para la censura, es cortedad. Emplearse todo en alabarlo, es desigual precio. Comencar en obediencia de registro, y acabar en pasmos de lo admirable, mas que obsequio, es necessidad: Si como Censor comencé, acabaré como quien suplica a V. A. Con el Imperio Real no sólo permita, no sólo alarque la licencia, sino con el medio más provido de su dictamen oblique a que sin tardanza veamos el día mas feliz desta impressión: Donde puedan los mortales descubrir las sendas de la eternidad entre las letras de este Sol, que nace para nuestra alegría; donde nuestra ingratitud encuentre con las verdades del agradecimiento, y nuestro ahogo con las medianera de los mejores alientos. Estaba en sombras de profecias escondido el prodigio de la Santidad de María. Salga a desempeño de nuestro consuelo en el principio de esta ensenanca, y a los que en las sombras de la muerte nunca merecimos ver la luz de la infinita misericordia executada en la única Emperatriz de Cielo, se nos da a conocer en el peligroso camino de esta mortalidad para hazer camino de paz la vida temporal que antes era riesgo, llena de tropiecos, y escándalos. Sumo es el provecho de esta lectura. Glorioso el deleyte de este novedad de milagros, que se refieren en la vida de nuestra Reyna María. Propríssimo es el estilo entre tantas luzes. Raro y eficáz es el rayo de su persuasión. Todo con sumo aprovechamiento a la seguridad católica. Argumento evidentíssimo de nuestra ingratitud para convencernos al desengaño. Salga a luz, pues la aumenta. No se detenga, pues nos importa. Y sirva de remedio al siglo para quien nació, que adolece de tan mortales achaques, Assí lo siento, y siento mas no tener toda la Sabiduría Angélica para significar mi aprecio, mi veneración, mi deseo. En San Martín de Madrid de la Religión de N.P.S. Benito a quinze de Dicembre de mil seiscientos y sesenta y seis años.

El Maestro Fray Diego de Silva.

Appendix III

This appendix contains the English translation of chapter titles of *La Mística Ciudad de Dios*, as well as official ecclesiastical "approbations", concerning the work found in an English translation from the French by: The Abbe Joseph A. Boullan published in 1872. (pages 132-142).

The remainder of this appendix includes the English translation of titles and approbations by Fiscar Morison published in 1914.

The purpose of Appendix III is to give an example of the common information prefacing most English translations that are readily available at the present date.

As does Appendix I, this third and last appendix also serves as an example of the extensive detail found in Sor María's account of this "Historia de la vida de la Virgen".

Divine Life of
The Most Holy Virgin Mary
Being an Abridgment of the
Mystical City of God
by Mary of Jesus of Agreda
1602-1665

by
F. Bonaventure Amedeo De Caesare, M. C.
Consultor of the Sacred Congregation of the Index.
Translation from the French of
The Abbe Joseph A. Boullan,
Doctor in geology
Phildadephia:
1872
Peter F. Cunningham, Catholic Bookseller, 216 South Third Street

CHAPTER I
The Most Holy Virgin in the Divine Counsels.—Her Holy Parents
CHAPTER II
The Immaculate Conception of Mary.—Her Holy Exercise in Her Mother's Womb
CHAPTER III
The Happy Birth of Mary.—First Fruits of Her Marvelous Life

81

Approbations

The volume which we offer to the public under the title of "The Divine Life of the Blessed Virgin Mary," is a faithful abridgment, without change, alteration, or modification of the facts, taken entirely and literally from the celebrated work, "The Mystical City," by Mary of Jesus of Agreda. Therefore, all the approbations granted to that admirable book, may and ought to be applicable to this.

We append a summary of these divers approbations of which we can warrant the authenticity, having copied them from the acts of the process of the beatification and canonization of the above mentioned servant of God, Mary of Agreda.

1st. Approbation of the ordinary of the diocese wherein the servant of God died in the odor of sanctity, and also of the bishop of the place where the work was printed. The bishops are, as we all know according to the canon law, the first judges of books published within their jurisdiction.

2d. Approbation of the learned tribunal of the Inguisition in Spain, which, having examined the book word for word, authorized its publication and diffusion among the faithful.

3d. Approbation of theologians of all religious bodies, Benedictines, Carmelites, Dominicans, and Jesuits, called upon to examine the work. They have eulogized it in the highest terms, and recommended it as the fruit of the Spirit of God.

4th. Approbation of the most celebrated universities of foreign lands, Salamanca, Louvain, Toulouse, etc., which, after the most minute examination, have declared that the book contains nothing against faith or morals; they have exalted immeasurably, as Pope Benedict XIV expresses it in his decree of 1748. The university of Paris alone is an exception, because it was, at that time tainted with Jansenism, to which this work is so adverse.

5th. In fine, Pope Innocent XI, after having placed this work on the Index, August 4th, 1680 because, said the postulator of the cause of canonization, of the contests which it had raised, withdrew it himself three months later, November 9th, 1680. This last decree has the force of a universal law of the church, for in 1713, a bishop having forbidden declared his prohibition null, and obliged him to retract it, as being contrary to the decree on November 9th, 1681 which decree, said the Sacred congregation, has the power of a law throughout the universal church. We know it is the same in our days. Alexander VIII authorized the reading of this work "oraculo vive vocis". In 1704 clement IX forbade it to be placed on the Index, and it would be vain to seek for it among the forbidden books.

And in fine, in 1729, with the approbation of Benedict XIII, of happy memory, the Sacred congregation of Rites published a decree, which permits the faithful to read and retain it without any other examination. Therefore he, who, whatever may be his title, honor, or dignity, presumes to forbid the reading of this work, authorized by the Holy See, would be obliged to retract, even publicly, if necessary.

Thus the cause is decided; pious reader, accept the book, and read it without fear, for Rome, which cannot fail in its examination of doctrine, has spoken.

Words of Wisdom
From, city of God
1914
Academy Library Guild
Fresno, California
Translated by:
Fiscar Morison.

What the Universities of Europe, the Religious
Orders and Learned Men Say of the
"Ciudad de Dios."

Forty years after the first appearance of the "Ciudad de Dios" the great universities of Europe were called upon to give their opinion about this great work. All the faculties, except the Jansenistic members of the Sorbonne at Paris, published highest recommendations. At the same time the learned men and teachers of each religious order that maintained institutions of learning in Europe, were asked to contribute their opinions. The following religious orders complied: The Augustinians, Benedictines, Carmelites, Dominicans, Jesuits, Cistercians, Sasilians, Trinitarians, Mercedarians, Minims, Hieronymites, Premonstratensians, Reformed Augustinians, Theatines, Minors of the Regular clergy, all unanimously endorsing the favorable decision previously published by the University of Salmanca. To the approbation of nearly all the Universities and Religious Orders, were then added the high eulogiums of other learned men, great divines, bishops and princes of the church and of the Popes and the Roman congregations. As a sample of what these witnesses said concerning the wonderful "Ciudad de Dios," we here select the official approbation of the University of Louvain, one of the great Universities of Europe. After pointing out that God's power of giving private revelations to whom He chooses, must not be circumscribed, and after referring to some general rules in regard to private revelations, the document proceeds to say:

"Now, while abiding the decision of the church concerning the revelations, which are given us under the title of the city of God, we, having read the whole work, say and are of the opinion, that the faithful can read it without danger to their faith and without damage to the purity of morals; for there is not found anything within it, which could lead to relaxation or to indiscreet rigor; but on the contrary, we have come to the conclusion that it will be most useful for enlivening and augmenting the piety of the faithful, the veneration of the most holy Virgin, and the respect for the sacred mysteries."

"The strong and the weak, the wise and the ignorant, and in fine, all the world will gather richest fruit from the reading of these books: for they contain what is most sublime in theology and in a style so simple, easy and perspicuous that, in order to enter deeply into an understanding of the holy mysteries, no more is necessary than to read them with sound judgment." "Combined with this simplicity are found many doctrines and valid proofs, free from contradictions and not easily found in other writings. This History explains more than a thousand difficulties in holy Scripture, in a manner equally natural and wonderful. At every step are encountered exquisite interpretations, until now unknown, and which had been hidden beneath the mere letter, but are laid open in these writings and brought to the light. In short, the whole work is a beautiful web of scripture passages which, though spun from its different books, are directly and specially woven into a whole for the purpose intended by the Venerable Mother." "In addition thereto the instructions given by the most holy Virgin at the end of each chapter contain the purest morality, instruct, entertain, and at the same time sweetly inculcate the love of virtue and abhorrence of vice, painting them in the most vivid and natural colours. They do not only convince the intellect, but they contain such a special unction, that they enkindle a sacred ardor in the soul. In meditating upon them one certainly will experience a delight not met with in ordinary writings; and the more they are read the greater is the delight experienced. Finally, the whole work contains something so unwonted and attractive that, once begun, the reading of it can scarcely be relinquished."

87

"The novelty and variety found in these writings delight and recreate the reader beyond all that is pleasant in the world, at the same time instructing him and inspiring him with new fervor. All can easily persuade themselves that, if the interior life of Christ our Lord and of the most holy Virgin was not just as described in these books, it could certainly have been like it; and that it would have been well worthy of Them, if it was as it is there depicted. All that is there said is befitting the majesty and humility of Christ, and in correspondence with the holiness of the Virgin and the dignity of the Mother; since there is found nothing in the whole work which was not worthy of both one and the other.

"Notwithstanding all this, we should not at all wonder if the book met with men who are disposed to be critical; for what book is there which can hope to escape the opposition of the people of our times? God has not even provided that the sacred Scriptures should be free from such attack among the greater part of the learned of this world. The whole philosophy of the pagans causes them to join the number of those who are opposed to the cross of Christ crucified; and among that number are also the libertines of our day."

"Of course there are certain points in this work which might give rise to apparent difficulties, and some of them occurred, and do occur, to us. But, in accordance with what we have said of the excellence and usefulness of this work, we have come to the conclusion that these few passages must not hinder us from giving it the commendation already given; besides, we must confess that we might possibly be ourselves mistaken in making these objections."

"This seemed to us the most reasonable course, since in this book there is something more than human. Anything so excellent and sublime cannot be ascribed to an over-excited imagination, since the whole work is consistent throughout. Nor can it be believed to be the work of a perverted mind, for, with a constant equanimity, it treats of the most deeply hidden and abstruse matters without involving itself in any contradictions; though often also it descends to innumerable minute and particular circumstances."

"There are contained in this work such noble, such devout circumstantial and pertinent discourses, as cannot be the result of mere discursive thought. Nor can it be attributed to the demon; for, from beginning to end, it suggests and breathes nothing but humility, patience and endurance of hardships."

"Therefore, just as 'Ciudad' must without a doubt be attributed to the venerable Mother of Agreda, who is claimed as its author, so she cannot

88

have composed it without particular help from on high. Our conclusive opinion is, that the City of God, for the good of the public, and for the advantages to be derived therefrom, should be brought forth to the light. This is our judgment, which we submit entirely to the supreme decision of the Holy See, to whom alone belongs the right of finally judging such writings."

Louvain, 20th of July 1715

(Signed)
HERMANN DAMEN,
Doctor, Professor Ordinary and Regent of the Theological Faculty, Don of Saint Peter, President of the College of Arras, Censor of Books, etc.
ANTON PARRENTIER,
Doctor, Professor Ordinary, Regent of the Theological Faculty, President of the Great college of Theologians, etc.

Approbations

The first Pope officially to take notice of "Ciudad de Dios" was Pope Innocent XI, who, on July 3, 1686, in response to a series of virulent attacks and machinations of some members of the Sorbonne, known to be Jansenists, issued a breve permitting the publication and reading of the "Ciudad de Dios." Similar decrees were afterward issued by Popes Alexander VIII, Clement IX and Benedict XIII. These decrees were followed by two decrees of the Congregation of Rites, approved by Benedict XIV and Clement XIV, in which the authenticity of "Ciudad de Dios" as extant and written by th venerable Servant of God, Mary of Jesus, is officially established. The great pope Benedict XIII, when he was archbishop of Benevent, used these revelations as material for a series of sermons on the Blessed Virgin. On Sept. 26, 1713, the bishop of Ceneda, Italy, objecting to the publication of the "City of God," was premptorily ordered by the Holy Office to withdraw his objections as interfering with the decree of pope Innocent XI for the universal Church.

The process of canonization of Mary of Agreda was promoted by the Spanish bishops and other eminent men of the Church soon after her death in 1666. It has resulted so far in securing her the title of Vereabilis, thus clearing the way to her beatification, for which, let us hope, God will soon raise a promoter among the many pious and eminent men who hold in esteem her writings and have learned of her holy life and of the miracles wrought at her tomb.

The Redemptorist Fathers published a new German translation in 1885, which was approved and highly recommended by the Bishop of Ratisbon in the following terms:

"We take pleasure in giving our episcopal approbation to the annotated

90

translation of the Spanish original "Ciudad de Dios" of Mary of Jesus and recommend this book, which will surely edify all readers and be the occasion of great spiritual blessings."

Ratisbon, September 29, 1885.

+ Ignatius, Bishop of Ratisbon.

Notable is the high recomendation of the Prince-Archbishop of Salzburg, Apost. Legate, Primate of Germany, etc.

"According to the decrees of Pope Innocent XI and Clement XI the book known as "Ciudad de Dios' written by the Venerable servant of God, Maria de Jesus, may be read by all the faithful."

"A number of episcopal approbations, the recommendations of four renowned universities, namely, of Toulouse, Salamanca, Alcala and Louvain, and of prominent members of different orders, coincide in extolling the above-named work. The learned and pious Cardinal D'Aguirre says that he considers all the studies of fifty years of his previous life as of small consequence in comparison with the doctrines he found in this book, which in all things are in harmony with the Holy scriptures, the Holy Fathers and Councils of the Church. The venerable superior-General of St. Sulpice, Abbe Emery, adds: "Only since I read the revelations of Mary of Agreda do I properly know Jesus and his Holy Mother."

"We therefore do not hesitate—in granting our episcopal approbation to—"Ciudad de Dios"—and wish to recommend it to the faithful and especially to our clergy."

Franz Albert,

Archbishop

Archiepiscopal Chancery, Salzburg.

September 12, 1885.

A more recent official approbation of "Ciudad de Dios" is from the Bishop of Tarazona, prefacing the new edition of 1911-1912.

"We, Dr. James Ozoidi y Udave, by the grace of God and of the Apostolic See, Bishop of Tarazona, Administrator Apostolic of the Diocese of Tudela, etc., etc.

Having charged the priest Don Eduardo Royo, chaplain and confessor at the convent of the Immaculate Conception of Agreda, carefully and exactly to compare the manuscript which is to serve as copy for the printing of the new edition of the "City of God" now about to be published by the religious of the above-named convent, with the authenticated autograph manuscript of that work there preserved, and having ascertained by a personal revision

91

of a great part of the manuscript that the said priest has diligently and faithfully fulfilled this charge imposed upon him by us:

We now therefore certify that this present edition of 'Ciudad de Dios,' with the exception of a few more orthographic modifications, is entirely conformable to the autograph of that work as composed and written by the venerable Mother Mary of Jesus of Agreda.

Tarazona, April 7, 1911.

[Diocesan seal]   + JAMES, Bishop of Tarazona

Finally follows the official approbation of the Right Reverend Bishop of the Fort Wayne Diocese, where this English translation is published.

Rome City, Inc., Aug. 24, 1912.

The Rev. George J. Blatter,

Dear Rev. Father: —

My Imprimatur is herewith granted to your English translation of the work entitled 'Ciudad de Dios.' Wishing you every blessing, I remain,

Devotedly in Domino,

+ H. J. ALERDING, Bishop of Fort Wayne.

The author has made use of capital letters in the text slightly at variance with common usage, in order to avoid complication and secure greater clearness. The paragraph numbers are those of the newest Spanish edition of "Ciudad de Dios" in 1912. In the abridgement they vary slightly.

City of God is divided into three Parts and eight Books. Part I contains Books 1 and 2. Part II contains Books 3, 4, 5, and 6. Part III contains Books 7 and 8. As circumstances compel a serial publication of the four volumes, the author judged it best to head these divisions as follows:

THE CONCEPTION, Books 1 and 2.
THE INCARNATION, Books 3 and 4.
THE TRANSFIXION, Books 5 and 6.
THE CORONATION, Books 7 and 8.

Scripta Humanistica

Directed by
BRUNO M. DAMIANI
The Catholic University of America
COMPREHENSIVE LIST OF PUBLICATIONS*

65. Michael Zappala, *Lucian of Samosata in the Two Hesperias:*
     An Essay in Literary and Cultural Translation. $49.50
66. Oscar Bonifaz, *Remembering Rosario: A Personal Glimpse in-*
     to the Life and Works of Rosario Castellanos. Translated and
     Edited by Myralyn F. Allgood. Foreword by Oscar Bonifaz.
     Prologue by Edward Terry. $27.50
67. *The Other Voices: Essays on Italian Regional Culture and*
     Language. Ed. John Staulo. $35.50
68. Mario Aste, *Grazia Deledda: Ethnic Novelist.* $38.50

BOOK ORDERS

* Clothbound. *All book orders,* except library orders, must be prepaid and addressed to **Scripta Humanistica**, 1383 Kersey Lane, Potomac, Maryland 20854. *Manuscripts* to be considered for publication should be sent to the same address.